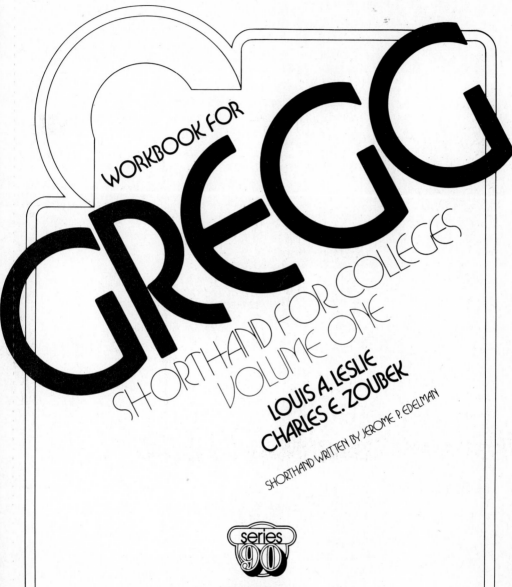

WORKBOOK FOR

GREGG

SHORTHAND FOR COLLEGES
VOLUME ONE

LOUIS A. LESLIE
CHARLES E. ZOUBEK

SHORTHAND WRITTEN BY JEROME P. EDELMAN

series 90

Gregg Division
McGraw-Hill Book Company

New York / Atlanta / Dallas / St. Louis / San Francisco / Auckland
Bogotá / Düsseldorf / Johannesburg / London / Madrid
Mexico / Montreal / New Delhi / Panama / Paris / São Paulo
Singapore / Sydney / Tokyo / Toronto

**Workbook for Gregg Shorthand
for Colleges, Volume One, Series 90**

Copyright © 1980, 1973, 1965, 1958 by
McGraw Hill, Inc. All Rights Reserved.
Copyright 1953 by McGraw Hill, Inc. All
Rights Reserved. Printed in the United
States of America. No part of this publica-
tion may be reproduced, stored in a re-
trieval system, or transmitted, in any form
or by any means, electronic, mechanical,
photocopying, recording, or otherwise,
without the prior written permission of the
publisher.

11 12 13 14 15 DODO 8 9 8 7 6

ISBN 0-07-037751-0

Your Workbook

Workbook for Gregg Shorthand for Colleges, Volume One, Series 90, has five major objectives, each designed to help you become an efficient stenographer or secretary, who can take dictation at a rapid rate and turn out mailable letters, correctly punctuated and without misspellings or errors in grammar.

These objectives are:

1   To develop your ability to build new words from those that you already know and to construct readable outlines for unfamiliar words.

2   To increase your vocabulary; the larger the number of words that are familiar to you, the more efficient secretary you will be.

3   To improve your ability to spell.

4   To improve your ability to punctuate.

5   To improve your mastery of English grammar.

If you practice the drills in this workbook faithfully, you will be delighted with the way your shorthand skill will grow and your ability to handle the mechanics of English will improve.

Practice procedures

EVOLUTION DRILLS

In Part 1 you will devote most of your practice in each lesson to Evolution Drills. The purpose of these drills is to help you construct shorthand outlines for new words from shorthand outlines that you already know.

In the Evolution Drills you will be given the shorthand outline for the first item. Using that outline as a guide, you are to fill in the shorthand outlines for the rest of the items on the line.

Examples

Words

In the workbook you will find:

safe   -s   save   -s   see   -s

or

hope   -s   -ing   -d

The completed drills will look like this:

safe   -s   save   -s   see   -s

or

hope   -s   -ing   -d

Word Beginnings

In the workbook you will find:

inside   -deed   -vite   -viting

*All the items on the line are to be based on the underscored syllable, word, or phrase.

The completed drill will look like this:

inside   -deed   -vite   -viting

Word Endings

In the workbook you will find:

neatly   nice-   on-   great-

The completed drill will look like this:

neatly   nice-   on-   great-

Phrases

In the workbook you will find:

in _the_   ⌐   -this   -that   -our

or

in _the_   ⌐   on-   with-   at-

The completed drills will look like this:

in _the_   ⌐   -this ⌐   -that ⌐   -our ⌐

or

in _the_   ⌐   on- ⌐   with- ⌐   at- ⌐

Practice the Evolution Drills in this way:

1 Spell and read aloud the shorthand outline that introduces each drill; thus, "s-a-f, safe." (Do not, however, spell brief forms and phrases; simply read them aloud without spelling.)

2 Write the shorthand outlines for the remaining items on the line, saying each word or phrase aloud as you write.

3 Whenever you encounter a form for which you cannot immediately construct an outline, write something and proceed at once to the next outline.

4 The next day in class consult your teacher or your classmates about any outlines that gave you trouble.

OTHER DRILLS

Instructions for practicing the other types of drills in Part 1 are given at the point where they are first introduced.

TIME GOALS

Shorthand, to be of value, must be written and read rapidly. The quicker you can finish each lesson (always writing legible shorthand, of course!), the more benefit you will derive from it—and the sooner you will be through with your assignment.

Therefore, you should set a goal for the completion of each lesson in this workbook. Here are some time goals for Part 1:

Lessons 1 through 6	12 minutes
Lessons 7 through 12	10 minutes
Lessons 13 through 18	9 minutes
Lessons 19 through 24	8 minutes
Lessons 25 through 30	7 minutes

You should be able to achieve these goals if you follow the practice suggestions that have been outlined for you.

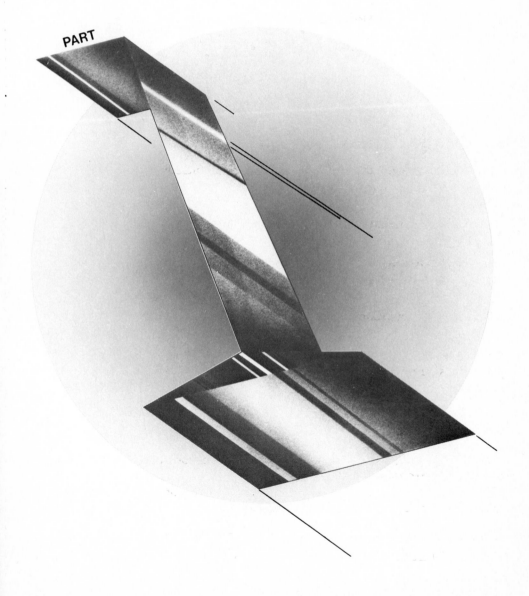

PART

Lessons 1-30

ALPHABET REVIEW
Here are the shorthand strokes you studied in Lessons 1 through 3. Below each shorthand letter, write its longhand meaning.

/ / _ __ ∘) ,) ○

....

ι ∪ . ○ ∪ ⟨ ⟨ (

....

BRIEF FORMS
A number of brief forms have more than one meaning. In each of the following sentences, a brief form that has more than one meaning is written in shorthand. In the space provided, transcribe the meaning that is correct.

Correct Transcript   Correct Transcript

1 *She visited* ∪ *store.* ....   6 *We will go in an* ∪ . ...

2 *I will* _ *drive.* ....   7 *She said I was* _ *late.* ....

3 *He owns* . *house.* ....   8 *Lee is not* ∪ . ...

4 *The students* ∪ *here.* ....   9 *He* ∪ *leave soon.* ....

5 *She will stay* / *home.* ....   10 *See me* _ *an hour.* ....

EVOLUTION DRILLS
Be sure to follow the instructions on page 5 of this workbook when you practice these drills.

1 *read*   -ing   -r   -s

2 *lead*   -s   -ing   -r

3 *stay*   -s   -ed   -ing

4 *deal*   -ing   -s   -r

5 *drive*   -r   -ing   -s

6 type   -ing   -s   -d

7 post   -s   -ing   -r

8 own   -r   -ing   -s

9 vote   -s   -r   -ing

10 hope   -ing   -s   -d

11 free   -s   -ing   -d

12 save   -ing   -s   -d

13 write   -r   -ing   -s

14 heat   -r   -s   -ing

15 near   -s   -ing   -r

16 trade   -ing   -s   -r

17 hear   -s   -ing   -r

18 _indeed_   -side   -vite   -viting

Phrases

19 _I_ have   -will   -am   -know

20 will not   I-   he-   it-

21 will not have   he-   I-   it-

22 I will   -not   he will   -not

12

ALPHABET REVIEW
Underneath each shorthand letter, write its longhand meaning.

EVOLUTION DRILLS
In the spaces provided, write the correct shorthand forms.

1 *weigh*   -ing   -s   -ed

2 *wait*   -s   -ing   -r

3 *sweet*   -s   -r

4 *wide*   -r   *wave*   -s

5 *waste*   -ing   -s

6 *beat*   -ing   -s   -r

7 *prove*   -s   -ing   -d

8 *move*   -s   -ing   -r

9 *rule*   -s   -ing   -r

10 cry ~~ -s   -ing   -d

11 keep ~~ -s   -ing   -r

12 take ~~ -s   -ing   -n

13 hide ~~ -s   -ing

14 grade ~~ -s   -ing   -r

15 greet ~~ -s   -ing   -r

16 know ~~ -s   -ing

17 like ~~ -s   -ing   -d

18 cool ~~ -s   -ing   -r

19 room ~~ -s   -ing   -r

20 suit ~~ -s   -ing

Phrases

21 <u>we</u> are ~~ -will   -have   -may

22 we do ~~ -not   I do ~~ -not

23 <u>we</u> mean ~~ -might   -need   -make

24 <u>who</u> are ~~ -will   -may   -have

25 <u>to</u> go ~~ -take   -try   -it

26 do not ~~ we-   who-

ALPHABET REVIEW

In Lessons 1 through 5 you have already studied more than half the strokes of Gregg Shorthand. See how well you remember those strokes by writing the longhand meaning underneath each shorthand stroke.

BRIEF FORMS

Transcribe the correct meaning of each brief form that is written in shorthand in the following sentences.

	Correct Transcript			Correct Transcript
1 We have ⟩ book.	....		6 Will ⌒ call me?	....
2 Did you pay ⌒ bill?	....		7 He leaves ╱ 10 p.m.	....
3 She ⟩ leaving now.	....		8 Jane may — finish.	....
4 When ‿ I see you?	....		9 I think he ⟩ right.	....
5 I know her ‿ .	....		10 Take ⌒ time.	....

EVOLUTION DRILLS

In the spaces provided, write the correct shorthand forms.

1 give   -s   -ing   -n

2 infer   -ing   -s   -ence

3 earn   -er   -ing   -s

15

4 *act*   -s   -r   -ing

5 *park*   -s   -ing   -ed

6 *bathe*   -ing   -s   -d

7 *smooth*   -s   -r   -ing

8 *throw*   -ing   -n   -s

9 *bill*   -s   -ing

10 *settle*   -r   -s   -ing

11 *win*   -ing   -s   -r

12 *invest*   -r   -s   -ing

13 *sweat*   -s   -r   -ing

14 *arrive*   -s   -ing   -d

15 *start*   -s   -r   -ing

Phrases

16 <u>you</u> *can*   -have   -will   -are

17 *if* <u>the</u>   in-   at-   to-

18 <u>of</u> *the*   -these   -that   -our

19 <u>we</u> *can*   -will   -will not   -have

20 <u>that</u> *have*   -is   -the   -are

16

RECALL

ALPHABET REVIEW

Under each shorthand letter, write its longhand meaning. Can you complete this alphabet review in 45 seconds or less?

/ / — — ₒ)) , ○

....

ᴜ ᴜ ᴜ • ○ ⟨ ((

....

⌒ ⌒ ⌒ ⌒ ⟋ ⟍

....

BRIEF FORMS

In the following sentences, transcribe the underscored brief form.

Correct Transcript   **Correct Transcript**

1 ....   4 ....

2 ....   5 ....

3 ....   6 ....

EVOLUTION DRILLS

In the spaces provided, write the correct shorthand forms.

1 *approve*   -s   -d   -al

2 *win*   -r   -s   -ing

3 *plan*   -s   -ing   -r

4 *grow*   -s   -ing   -r

5 *scheme*   -s   -ing   -r

17

6 travel ⟨shorthand⟩ -s   -ing   -r

7 remove ⟨shorthand⟩ -s   -ing   -d

8 glue ⟨shorthand⟩ -s   -ing   -d

9 invite ⟨shorthand⟩ -ing   -s

10 appear ⟨shorthand⟩ -s   -ing   -ance

11 agree ⟨shorthand⟩ -s   -ing   -d

12 pave ⟨shorthand⟩ -s   -ing   -d

13 list ⟨shorthand⟩ -s   -ing   -less

14 back ⟨shorthand⟩ -s   -ing   -r

15 glance ⟨shorthand⟩ -ing   -d

16 mark ⟨shorthand⟩ -s   -ed   -ing

Phrases

17 <u>we</u> met ⟨shorthand⟩ -get   -do   -make

18 <u>we</u> will ⟨shorthand⟩ -are   -can   -may

19 <u>in</u> it ⟨shorthand⟩ -that   -the   -our

20 <u>with</u> him ⟨shorthand⟩ -the   -that   -these

21 <u>I</u> might ⟨shorthand⟩ -may   -can   -will

22 <u>you</u> do ⟨shorthand⟩ -will   -can   -may

LESSON

EVOLUTION DRILLS

In the spaces provided, write the correct shorthand forms.

1 *shop*   -ing   -s   -ed

2 *solve*   -s   -ing   -d

3 *borrow*   -s   -ed   -ing

4 *call*   -s   -r   -ing

5 *author*   -s   -ize   -ized

6 *stock*   -s   -ing   -ed

7 *occur*   -s   -ing   -ence

8 *small*   -r   *tall*   -r

9 *golf*   -s   -ing   -r

10 *lock*   -ing   -s   -ed

11 *talk*   -s   -ing   -ed

12 *draw*   -s   -ing   -r

13 *job*   -s   -r   -rs

14 *follow*   -s   -ing   -r

15 *dock*		-ing	-s	-ed
16 *charge*		-s	-d	-ing
17 *pledge*		-s	-ing	-d
18 *vote*		-s	-ing	-r
19 *spot*		-ing	-s	-less
20 *thought*		-s	-less	
21 *check*		-s	-ing	-ed
22 *ship*		-s	-ed	-ing
23 *insure*		-s	-ing	-r
24 *injure*		-s	-ing	-y
25 *sketch*		-ing	-s	-ed

Phrases

26 <u>on</u> it		-that	-the	-our
27 <u>to</u> talk		-go	-gain	-it
28 <u>you</u> may		-might	-can	-will
29 <u>we</u> thought		-will	-might	-can
30 <u>I</u> saw		-thought	-may	-can

BRIEF FORMS

In the following sentences, transcribe the correct meaning of each underscored brief form.

Correct Transcript | Correct Transcript

1 ⌐ᵖ (⌐ ⌐ 10 ⟍ .... 4 ℯ ⁄ ⁀ ⁄ᵣ ⟍ ....

2 ⌒ ⌐ᵉ (7 × .... 5 ⌄ ⁖ ⟩ ! ....

3 ⟩ ⌐ᵉ ⁊ ⌐ᵉ ⟍ .... 6 ⌐ ⁄ ⌐ ℴᵣ·⌐ ⟍ ....

EVOLUTION DRILLS

In the spaces provided, write the correct shorthand forms.

1 begin   *-s*   *-ing*   *-r*

2 believe   *-ing*   *-s*   *-d*

3 <u>be</u>fore   *-cause*   *-came*   *-neath*

4 fair   *-ness*   *-r*   *-ly*

5 name   *-s*   *-ing*   *-ly*

6 near   *-r*   *-s*   *-ly*

7 clear   *-s*   *-r*   *-ly*

8 firm   *-s*   *-ly*   *-r*

9 open   *-s*   *-ing*   *-ly*

10 separate   *-ing*   *-s*   *-ly*

11 cost   *-s*   *-ly*   *-ing*

12 light   *-s*   *-ly*   *-r*

13 *brief* ⟋ -s -r -ly

14 *act* ⟋ -s -ive -ively

15 *like* ⟋ -s -d -ly

Phrases and Quantities

16 *I would* ⟋ we- you- who-

17 *there is* ⟋ -are -will -have

18 *for this* ⟋ -that -the -them

19 *by these* ⟋ -the -that -them

20 *800* ⟋ *300,000* *$600,000* *$900,000*

21 *4,000* ⟋ *3,000* *$3,000* *$6,000*

Recall

22 *thought* ⟋ -s -less

23 *fill* ⟋ -s -ing -r

24 *hurry* ⟋ -s -ing -ed

25 *learn* ⟋ -s -ing -r

26 *wire* ⟋ -s -ing -less

27 *bill* ⟋ -s -ing

28 *give* ⟋ -s -ing -n

29 *thin* ⟋ -r *thick* ⟋ -r

22

EVOLUTION DRILLS

In the spaces provided, write the correct shorthand forms.

1 *motion* _____   -s   -ing   -ed

2 *nation* _____   -s   -al   -ally

3 *occasion* _____   -s   -al   -ally

4 *caution* _____   -s   -ing   -ed

5 *option* _____   -s   -al   -ed

6 *install* _____   -s   -ation   -ations

7 *patient* _____   -s   -ly

8 *efficient* _____   -ly   *proficient* _____   -ly

9 *profession* _____   -s   -al   -als

10 *cancel* _____   -s   -ing   -ation

11 *prepare* _____   -s   -ation   -ations

12 *operation* _____   -s   -al

13 *ration* _____   -s   -ing   -al

14 *section* _____   -s   -al   -ed

Phrases

15 <u>to</u> see ✒   -say   -sell   -sail

16 <u>to</u> be ✒   -have   -pay   -blame

17 <u>to</u> place ✒   -prove   -please   -plan

18 <u>to</u> change ✒   -check   -charge   -choose

Recall

19 give<u>n</u> ✒   take-   prove-

20 lead<u>er</u> ✒   read-   farm-   late-

21 fear<u>less</u> ✒ harm-   thought-   need-

22 neat<u>ly</u> ✒   bare-   dear-   fair-

23 dear<u>est</u> ✒   near-   mere-   fine-

24 throw ✒   -ing   -s   -n

25 lock ✒   -s   -ing   -ed

26 swim ✒   -s   -ing   -r

27 search ✒   -ed   -ing   -s

28 wait ✒   -s   -ing   -r

29 move ✒   -d   -ing   -rs

30 broad ✒   -ly   -r

EVOLUTION DRILLS

In the spaces provided, write the correct shorthand forms.

1 grind   -s   -ing   -r

2 friend   -s   -ly   -less

3 bind   -s   -ing   -r

4 kind   -s   -ly   -r

5 end   -s   -ing   -less

6 grant   -s   -ing   -ed

7 rent   -s   -ing   -al

8 print   -s   -ing   -r

9 prevent   -s   -ing   -ed

10 indicate   -s   -ing   -r

11 notice   -s   -ing   -d

12 increase   -ing   -d   -s

13 cause   -s   -ing   -d

14 please   -s   -ing   -d

15 *address*		-s	-ing	-ed
16 *place*		-s	-ing	-d
17 *release*		-s	-ing	-d
18 *pass*		-s	-ing	-ed
19 *guess*		-s	-ing	-ed
20 *trace*		-s	-ing	-d
21 *own*		-s	-r	-ed
22 *line*		-s	-ing	-d
23 *paint*		-s	-ing	-r
24 *plan*		-s	-ing	-ed

Phrases

25 <u>into</u> that		-these	-the	-it
26 <u>to buy</u>		-find	-bind	-print
27 <u>there</u> may		-is	-are	-will
28 <u>by which</u>		-the	-that	-it
29 <u>for this</u>		-the	-that	-it
30 who <u>didn't</u>		I-	we-	you-

26

EVOLUTION DRILLS

In the spaces provided, write the correct shorthand forms.

1 *injure*   -s   -ing   -d

2 *offer*   -s   -ing   -ed

3 *favor*   -ing   -s   -ed

4 *wire*   -s   -ing   -d

5 *hire*   -ing   -s   -d

6 *occur*   -s   -ence   -ed

7 *assure*   -d   -s   -ance

8 *bill*   -s   -ing   -ed

9 *tire*   -s   -less   -d

10 *mail*   -ing   -s   -ed

11 *fail*   -ing   -s   -ed

12 *file*   -s   -ing   -d

13 *seal*   -s   -ing   -ed

14 *prepare*   -s   -ation   -d

15 *after* 〈shorthand〉   -math   -noon   -thought

16 *hand* 〈shorthand〉   -l   -ls   -y

17 *send* 〈shorthand〉   -s   -ing   -r

Phrases

18 *have been* 〈shorthand〉   you-   we-   who-

19 *have not been* 〈shorthand〉   you-   I-   who-

20 *have not been able* 〈shorthand〉   you-   I-   who-

21 *should be able* 〈shorthand〉   you-   I-   he-

22 *will be able* 〈shorthand〉   you-   we-   he-

23 *would be able* 〈shorthand〉   you-   I-   he-

24 *and* which 〈shorthand〉   -are   -will   -the

25 *could be* 〈shorthand〉   I-   he-   we-

26 *from these* 〈shorthand〉   -that   -our   -them

Recall

27 *center* 〈shorthand〉   -s   -ing

28 *sign* 〈shorthand〉   -s   -ing   -ed

29 *endorse* 〈shorthand〉   -s   -ing   -d

30 *finance* 〈shorthand〉   -s   -ing   -d

28

RECALL

BRIEF FORMS

In the space provided, write the correct meaning of each underscored brief form.

	Correct Transcript			Correct Transcript
1			6	
2			7	
3			8	
4			9	
5			10	

EVOLUTION DRILLS

In the spaces provided, write the correct shorthand forms.

		-r	-ing	-ed
1	call	-r	-ing	-ed
2	caution	-s	-ing	-ed
3	paint	-s	-ing	-r
4	centralize	-s	-ing	-d
5	indicate	-s	-ing	-r
6	oppose	-s	-ing	-d
7	propose	-s	-ing	-d
8	accord	-s	-ing	-ance
9	store	-s	-ing	-d
10	ignore	-s	-ing	-d

11 *hard*   -r   -est   -ly

12 *guard*   -s   -ing   -ed

13 *fold*   -r   -rs   -ed

14 *begin*   -s   -ing   -r

15 *cost*   -s   -ing   -ly

16 *proficient*   -ly   *efficient*   -ly

17 *brace*   -s   -ing   -d

Phrases

18 *have not been able*   we-   you-   who-

19 *will be able*   we-   you-   he-

20 *be able*   would-   should-   to-

21 <u>*into*</u> *these*   -that   -the   -this

22 <u>*to*</u> *pay*   -buy   -show   -place

23 *should be*   he-   I-   you-

24 <u>*from*</u> *which*   -the   -these   -this

25 *could not*   I-   you-   we-

26 *could be*   I-   he-   you-

27 *on* <u>*them*</u>   to-   with-   of-

EVOLUTION DRILLS
In the spaces provided, write the correct shorthand forms.

Brief Forms

1 *work* ⌒   -s   -ing   -ed

2 *enclose* ⌒   -s   -ing   -d

3 *glad* ⌒   -ly   -ness

4 *order* ⟋   -s   -ing   -ly

5 *soon* ⌐   -r   *circular* ⌒   -s

6 *thank* ⌒   -s   -ing   -ed

Phrases

7 *thank you* ⌒   -for   -for the   -for your

8 *I was* ⌒   he-   there-   it-

9 *be glad* ⌒   I will-   you will-   we will-

10 *I enclosed* ⌒   we-   who-   you-

11 *send us* ⌒   from-   with-   for-

12 *does not* ⌒   he-   this-   who-

13 *I must* ⌒   he-   we-   you-

14 *in order* ⟋   -that   -that the

Words

15 *color* ⌒⌒   -s   -ing   -ed

16 *cover* ⁊   -ing   -s   -ed

17 *book* ⌐   -s   -ing   -ed

18 *full* ⅃   -r   -fill

19 *adjust* ⌇   -s   -ing   -r

20 *hunt* ⌇   -r   -s   -ing

21 *look* ⌣⌐   -s   -ing   -ed

22 *number* ⌐⁊   -s   -ed   -ing

23 *suffer* ⌇   -s   -ing   -ed

24 *pull* ⌐   -ing   -ed

BUSINESS VOCABULARY BUILDER

Write the underscored words in longhand; then define them briefly.

1 ....

2 ....

3 ....

EVOLUTION DRILLS

In the spaces provided, write the correct shorthand forms.

1 *quick*   -r   -ness   -ly

2 *quote*   -s   -ing   -d

3 *equip*   -s   -ing   -ed

4 *square*   -s   -d   -ly

5 *insert*   -s   -ing   -ed

6 *indicate*   -ing   -s   -d

7 *study*   -s   -ed   -ing

8 *deduct*   -s   -ing

9 *audit*   -ing   -s   -r

10 *credit*   -s   -ing   -r

11 *grade*   -s   -ing   -d

12 *need*   -s   -ed   -less

13 *test*   -s   -ing   -ed

14 *act*   -s   -r   -ed

15 rate ___   -ing   -s   -d

16 wait ___   -r   -rs   -ed

17 guide ___   -ing   -s   -d

18 list ___   -s   -ing   -ed

19 date ___   -ing   -s   -d

20 note ___   -s   -ing   -d

21 lift ___   -s   -ing   -ed

22 provide ___   -s   -r   -d

23 accept ___   -s   -ing   -ed

24 operate ___   -s   -r   -d

25 omit ___   -s   -ing   -ed

BUSINESS VOCABULARY BUILDER

Write the underscored words in longhand; then define them briefly.

1 ___

....

2 ___

....

3 ___

....

EVOLUTION DRILLS

In the spaces provided, write the correct shorthand forms.

Brief Forms

1 *business* ⌇   -s   -like

2 *any* ⟋   -one   -thing   -body

3 *value* ⟍   -s   -less   -ble

4 *think* ⌐·   -s   -ing

Phrases

5 <u>about</u> it ℓ   -that   -this   -your

6 *they* <u>think</u> ⌐·   we-   who-   you-

7 <u>what</u> has ⅆ   -is   -will   -are

8 *any* <u>one</u> ⟋   each-   this-

Words

9 *table* ℓ   -s   -ing   -d

10 *cable* ℘   -s   -ing   -d

11 *adjust* ⟋   -ing   -ed   -ble

12 *profit* ⟋   -s   -ed   -ble

13 *reason* ⟋   -s   -ing   -ble

14 *receive* 　-s　　　　-ing　　　　-d

15 *repair*　　-s　　　　-ing　　　　-ed

16 *refer*　　-s　　　　-ed　　　　-ence

17 *resign*　　-s　　　　-ing　　　　-ed

18 *resist*　　-s　　　　-ing　　　　-ed

19 *repeat*　　-s　　　　-ing　　　　-ed

20 *accept*　　-s　　　　-ed　　　　-ble

21 *agree*　　-s　　　　-d　　　　-ble

22 *rely*　　-s　　　　-ing　　　　-ble

23 *replace*　　-s　　　　-ing　　　　-ble

24 *adapt*　　-ed　　　　-ing　　　　-ble

BUSINESS VOCABULARY BUILDER
Write the underscored words in longhand; then define them briefly.

1

. . . .

2

. . . .

3

. . . .

. . . .

EVOLUTION DRILLS

In the spaces provided, write the correct shorthand forms.

1 *toil* ~~~~   -ing   -s   -ed

2 *annoy* ~~~~   -ance   -d   -ing

3 *point* ~~~~   -ing   -less   -s

4 *appoint* ~~~~   -s   -ing   -ed

5 *manage* ~~~~   -s   -ing   -d

6 *mention* ~~~~   -ing   -s   -ed

7 *fresh* ~~~~   -ly   -ness   -men

8 *mend* ~~~~   -s   -ing   -ed

9 *meant* ~~~~   -al   -ally

10 *year* ~~~~   -s   *yarn* ~~~~   -s

11 *yell* ~~~~   -s   -ing

12 *yield* ~~~~   -s   -ing   -ed

13 *eliminate* ~~~~   -s   -d

14 *administer* ~~~~   -s   -ing   -ation

15 *oil* 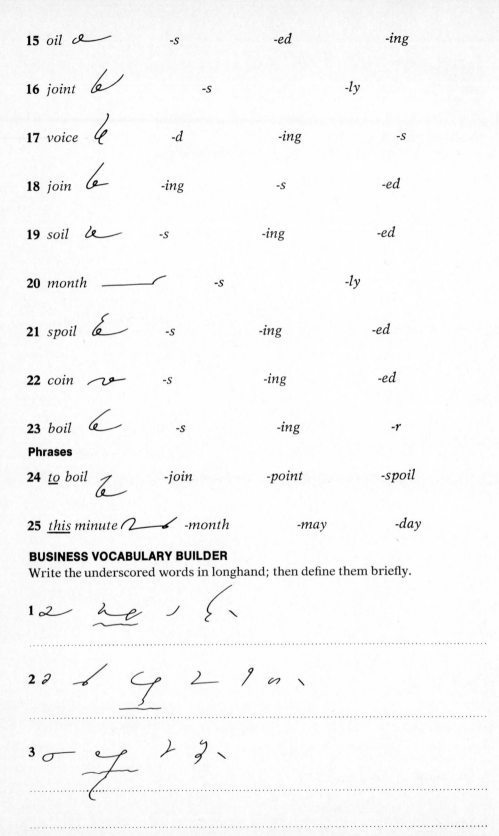   -s   -ed   -ing

16 *joint*   -s   -ly

17 *voice*   -d   -ing   -s

18 *join*   -ing   -s   -ed

19 *soil*   -s   -ing   -ed

20 *month*   -s   -ly

21 *spoil*   -s   -ing   -ed

22 *coin*   -s   -ing   -ed

23 *boil*   -s   -ing   -r

Phrases

24 <u>to</u> *boil*   -join   -point   -spoil

25 <u>this</u> *minute*   -month   -may   -day

BUSINESS VOCABULARY BUILDER

Write the underscored words in longhand; then define them briefly.

1

....

2

....

3

....

38

EVOLUTION DRILLS
In the spaces provided, write the correct shorthand forms.

Brief Forms

1 *manufacture* _____ -s   -ing   -r

2 *short*   -ly   -r   -hand

3 *where*   -by   -in   -abouts

4 *accompany*   -s   -ing   -ed

Phrases

5 <u>next month</u>   -year   -morning

6 <u>to persuade</u>   -purchase   -permit   -perfect

7 <u>per minute</u>   -hour   -month

Words

8 *permit*   -s   -ed   -ing

9 *perfect*   -s   -ed   -ly

10 *person*   -s   -al   -ally

11 *persuade*   -s   -d   -ing

12 *purchase*   -ing   -r   -rs

13 *decide*   -s   -ing   -d

14 *direct* 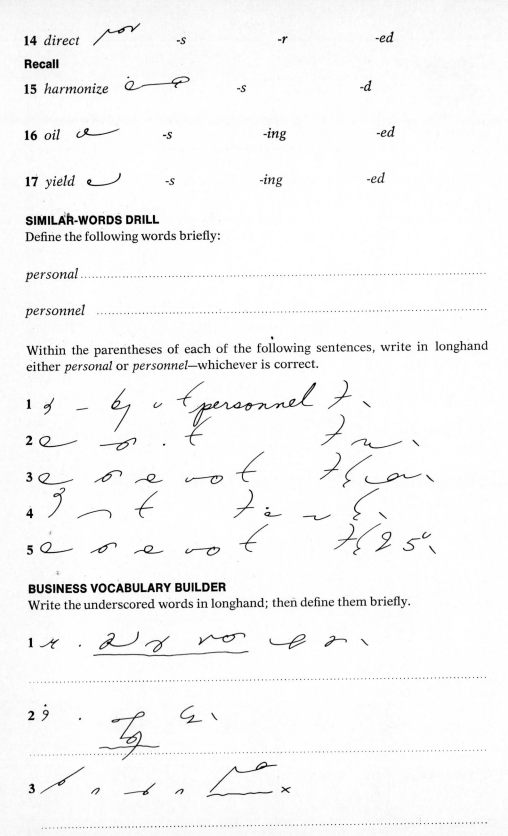 -s -r -ed

Recall

15 *harmonize* -s -d

16 *oil* -s -ing -ed

17 *yield* -s -ing -ed

SIMILAR-WORDS DRILL

Define the following words briefly:

personal..

personnel ....

Within the parentheses of each of the following sentences, write in longhand either *personal* or *personnel*—whichever is correct.

1

2

3

4

5

BUSINESS VOCABULARY BUILDER

Write the underscored words in longhand; then define them briefly.

1

....

2

....

3

....

RECALL

EVOLUTION DRILLS

In the spaces provided, write the correct shorthand forms.

Brief Forms

1 *work* ⌒   -ed   -s   -ing

2 *order* ✓   -s   -ly   -ing

3 *enclose* ⌐   -ing   -d   -s

4 *value* ⌡   -s   -ble   -bles

5 *glad* ⌒   -ly   -ness

6 *manufacture* ⌐   -d   -r   -rs

7 *short* ✓   -r   -est   -ly

8 *business* ⌠   -s   -like

Phrases

9 *any* <u>one</u> ⌐   only-   each-   which-

10 *thank you for* ⌐   -the   -this   -your

11 <u>about</u> *that* ⌐   -the   -this   -them

12 <u>what will</u> ⌐   -was   -is   -are

13 *does not* ⌐   this-   he-   who-

14 I _think_ 〈shorthand〉   you-   who-   to-

Words

15 mention 〈shorthand〉   -s   -ing   -ed

16 depend 〈shorthand〉   -s   -ent   -ing

17 persuade 〈shorthand〉   -s   -d   -ing

18 quote 〈shorthand〉   -s   -d   -ing

19 direct 〈shorthand〉   -s   -ly   -ed

20 look 〈shorthand〉   -s   -ing   -ed

21 reason 〈shorthand〉   -s   -ing   -ble

22 detail 〈shorthand〉   -s   -ing   -ed

23 join 〈shorthand〉   -s   -ing   -ed

24 purchase 〈shorthand〉   -ing   -r   -d

BUSINESS VOCABULARY BUILDER

Write the underscored words in longhand; then define them briefly.

1 〈shorthand〉

....

2 〈shorthand〉

....

3 〈shorthand〉

....

42

EVOLUTION DRILLS

In the spaces provided, write the correct shorthand forms.

Brief Forms

1 *present* $\mathcal{C}$ -s   -ed   -ing

2 *represent* $\mathcal{Z}$ -ing   -s   -ed

3 *part* $\mathcal{L}$ -ly   -s   -ing

4 *depart* $\mathcal{L}$ -s   -ing   -ment

5 *advertise*   -s   -ment   -ing

Words

6 *initial*   -s   -ing   -ed

7 *special*   -s   -ize   -ist

8 *official*   -s   -ly

9 *essential*   -s   -ly

10 *unite*   -s   -ing   -d

11 *review*   -ed   -ing   -s

12 *refuse*   -ing   -d   -s

13 *accuse*   -d   -ing   -s

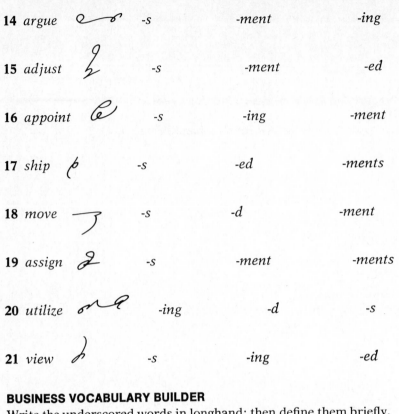

14 *argue*   -s   -ment   -ing

15 *adjust*   -s   -ment   -ed

16 *appoint*   -s   -ing   -ment

17 *ship*   -s   -ed   -ments

18 *move*   -s   -d   -ment

19 *assign*   -s   -ment   -ments

20 *utilize*   -ing   -d   -s

21 *view*   -s   -ing   -ed

BUSINESS VOCABULARY BUILDER

Write the underscored words in longhand; then define them briefly.

1 ....

2 ....

SPELLING REVIEW

Transcribe the following words in longhand, being careful to spell them correctly. They appear in the margins of the Reading and Writing Practice of Lesson 19 of your text.

1 ....   5 ....

2 ....   6 ....

3 ....   7 ....

4   8

EVOLUTION DRILLS

In the spaces provided, write the correct shorthand forms.

1 *found*　　　　-r　　　　　　　-ed　　　　　　　-ry

2 *doubt*　　　　-s　　　　　　　-less　　　　　　-ed

3 *allow*　　　　-s　　　　　　　-ing　　　　　　-ance

4 *announce*　　　-ing　　　　　　-s　　　　　　　-ment

5 *gather*　　　　-s　　　　　　　-ing　　　　　　-ed

6 *lather*　　　　-s　　　　　　　-ing　　　　　　-ed

7 *bother*　　　　-s　　　　　　　-ing　　　　　　-ed

8 *brother*　　　　　-s　　　　　　　　　　-ly

9 *confer*　　　　-s　　　　　　　-ed　　　　　　-ence

10 *consist*　　　　-s　　　　　　-ing　　　　　　-ed

11 *consign*　　　-ing　　　　　　-s　　　　　　　-ed

12 *consider*　　　-s　　　　　　　-ed　　　　　　-ble

13 *complain*　　　-s　　　　　　　-ed　　　　　　-ing

14 *complete*　　　-s　　　　　　　-d　　　　　　　-ly

45

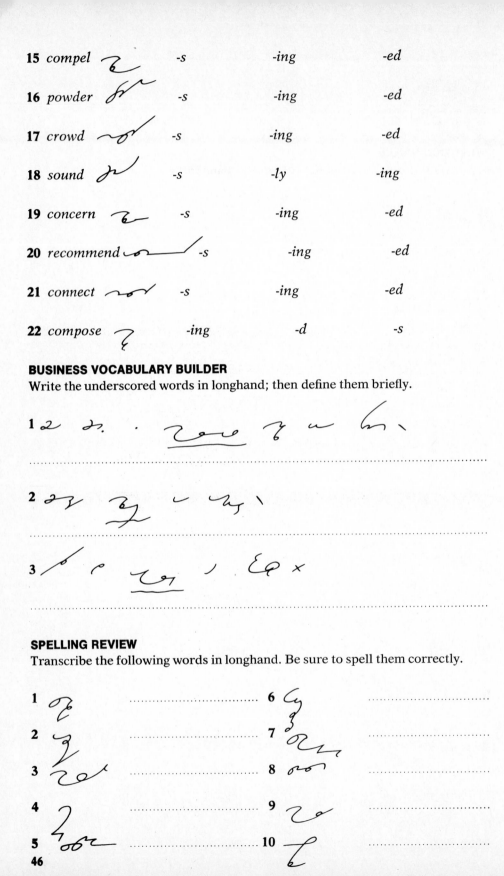

15 *compel*   -s   -ing   -ed

16 *powder*   -s   -ing   -ed

17 *crowd*   -s   -ing   -ed

18 *sound*   -s   -ly   -ing

19 *concern*   -s   -ing   -ed

20 *recommend*   -s   -ing   -ed

21 *connect*   -s   -ing   -ed

22 *compose*   -ing   -d   -s

BUSINESS VOCABULARY BUILDER

Write the underscored words in longhand; then define them briefly.

1

....

2

....

3

....

SPELLING REVIEW

Transcribe the following words in longhand. Be sure to spell them correctly.

1   6

2   7

3   8

4   9

5   10

46

EVOLUTION DRILLS

In the spaces provided, write the correct shorthand forms.

Brief Forms

1 *suggest*	-s	-ing	-ed
2 *every*	-thing	-one	-body
3 *out*	-side	-line	-let
4 *ever*	what-	where-	when-

Phrases

5 *every minute*	-month	-day	-one
6 *several days*	-months	-others	-minutes
7 *very well*	-little	-important	-glad

Words

8 *evident*	-ly	*confident*	-ly
9 *condense*	-s	-ing	-d
10 *abandon*	-s	-ing	-ed
11 *tend*	-ing	-s	-r
12 *identify*	-s	-ing	-ed
13 *attend*	-s	-ing	-ed

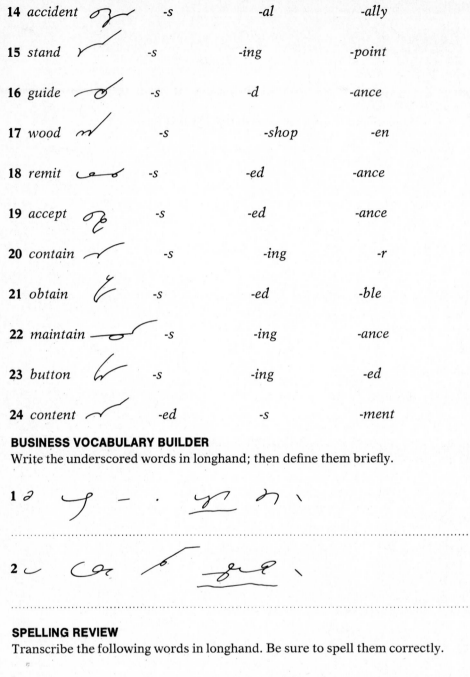

14 *accident*   -s   -al   -ally

15 *stand*   -s   -ing   -point

16 *guide*   -s   -d   -ance

17 *wood*   -s   -shop   -en

18 *remit*   -s   -ed   -ance

19 *accept*   -s   -ed   -ance

20 *contain*   -s   -ing   -r

21 *obtain*   -s   -ed   -ble

22 *maintain*   -s   -ing   -ance

23 *button*   -s   -ing   -ed

24 *content*   -ed   -s   -ment

BUSINESS VOCABULARY BUILDER

Write the underscored words in longhand; then define them briefly.

1 ....

2 ....

SPELLING REVIEW

Transcribe the following words in longhand. Be sure to spell them correctly.

1 ....   5 ....

2 ....   6 ....

3 ....   7 ....

4 ....   8 ....

EVOLUTION DRILLS

In the spaces provided, write the correct shorthand forms.

1 *damage*   -ing   -s   -d

2 *sel<u>dom</u>*   free-   ran-

3 *demonstrate*   -ing   -s   -d

4 *temper*   -s   -ed   -ary

5 *contemplate*   -s   -ing   -d

6 *estimate*   -s   -ing   -d

7 *custom*   -s   -r   -ary

8 *attempt*   -ing   -s   -ed

Phrases

9 *<u>to</u> know*   -make   -me

10 *<u>My dear</u> Mrs.*   -Ms.   -Miss

11 *<u>Dear</u> Mr.*   -Mrs.   -Miss

Days and Months

12 *Sunday*   *Tuesday*   *Friday*   *Saturday*

13 *January*   *August*   *December*   *October*

14 *Friday <u>morning</u>*   *Tuesday-*   *Thursday-*

Recall

15 *evident* 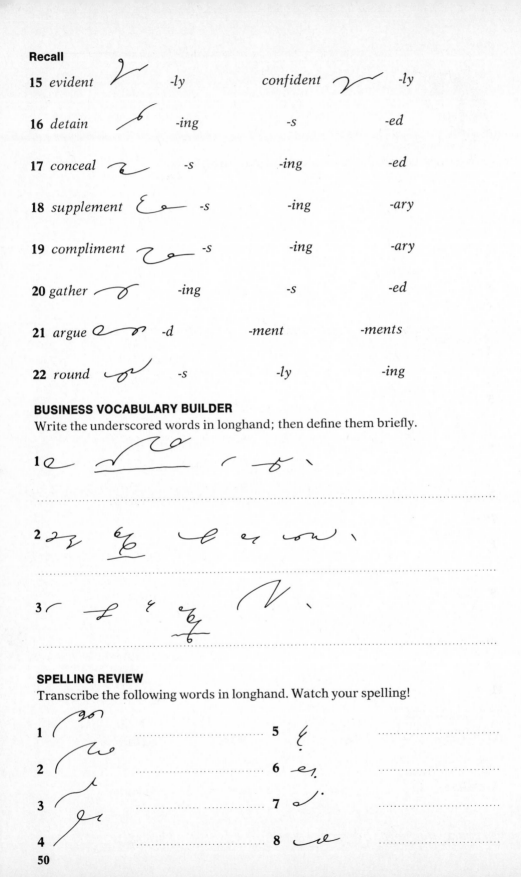 -ly   *confident*   -ly

16 *detain*   -ing   -s   -ed

17 *conceal*   -s   -ing   -ed

18 *supplement*   -s   -ing   -ary

19 *compliment*   -s   -ing   -ary

20 *gather*   -ing   -s   -ed

21 *argue*   -d   -ment   -ments

22 *round*   -s   -ly   -ing

BUSINESS VOCABULARY BUILDER

Write the underscored words in longhand; then define them briefly.

1 ....

2 ....

3 ....

SPELLING REVIEW

Transcribe the following words in longhand. Watch your spelling!

1 ....   5 ....

2 ....   6 ....

3 ....   7 ....

4   8

50

EVOLUTION DRILLS

In the spaces provided, write the correct shorthand forms.

Brief Forms

1 *over* ∪   *-do*   *-see*   *-look*

2 *overcharge*   *-s*   *-ing*   *-d*

3 *question*   *-s*   *-ed*   *-ble*

4 *time*   *-s*   *-d*   *-ing*

5 *general*   *-ly*   *-ize*   *-ized*

6 *organize*   *-ing*   *-d*   *-ation*

7 *acknowledge*   *-s*   *-ment*   *-ments*

Words

8 *defeat*   *-s*   *-ed*   *-ing*

9 *develop*   *-s*   *-ment*   *ments*

10 *devote*   *-ing*   *-s*   *-d*

11 *divert*   *-s*   *-ing*   *-ed*

12 *divide*   *-s*   *-r*   *-d*

13 *differ*   *-s*   *-ence*   *-ences*

14 *appreciate*   *-s*   *-ing*   *-d*

BUSINESS VOCABULARY BUILDER

Write the underscored words in longhand; then define them briefly.

1 _[shorthand]_

....

2 _[shorthand]_

....

3 _[shorthand]_

....

SIMILAR-WORDS DRILL

Define the following words briefly:

to *(preposition)* ....

too ....

two ....

Transcribe the underscored words in the spaces provided.

1 _[shorthand]_ ....

2 _[shorthand]_ ....

3 _[shorthand]_ ....

4 _[shorthand]_ ....

5 _[shorthand]_ ....

SPELLING REVIEW

Transcribe the following words in longhand.

1 _[shorthand]_ .... 5 _[shorthand]_ ....

2 _[shorthand]_ .... 6 _[shorthand]_ ....

3 _[shorthand]_ .... 7 _[shorthand]_ ....

4 _[shorthand]_ 8 _[shorthand]_

RECALL

EVOLUTION DRILLS

In the spaces provided, write the correct shorthand forms.

Brief Forms

1 *acknowledge* ⌒   -s   -ing   -ment

2 <u>*overstay*</u> ⌐ʋ   -do   -coat   -time

3 *question* ⌒   -s   -ed   -ble

4 *organize* ⌒   -d   -ing   -ation

5 *time* (-ly   -ing   -r

6 *general* ∠   -s   -ly   -ize

7 <u>*meantime*</u> ⌐○⌐   day-   noon-

8 *out* ○   -side   -live   -line

9 *every*)   -body   -where   -one

10 *suggest* ⌒   -s   -ing   -ed

11 *present* C   -s   -ing   -ly

12 *ever*)   when-   what-   where-

13 *part* C   -s   -ing   -ed

Words

14 *unite* ⟨shorthand⟩   -s   -ing   -d

15 *appreciate* ⟨shorthand⟩   -s   -ing   -d

16 *develop* ⟨shorthand⟩   -s   -ed   -ment

17 *definite* ⟨shorthand⟩   -ly   *different* ⟨shorthand⟩   -ly

18 *damage* ⟨shorthand⟩   -s   -d   -ing

19 *contain* ⟨shorthand⟩   -s   -ing   -r

20 *initiate* ⟨shorthand⟩   -s   -ing   -d

21 *compete* ⟨shorthand⟩   -s   -ing   -d

BUSINESS VOCABULARY BUILDER

Write the underscored words in longhand; then define them briefly.

1 ⟨shorthand outlines⟩

....

2 ⟨shorthand outlines⟩

....

3 ⟨shorthand outlines⟩

....

SPELLING REVIEW

Transcribe the following words. Watch your spelling!

1 ⟨shorthand⟩ ....   **5** ⟨shorthand⟩ ....

2 ⟨shorthand⟩ ....   **6** ⟨shorthand⟩ ....

3 ⟨shorthand⟩ ....   **7** ⟨shorthand⟩ ....

4 ⟨shorthand⟩ ....   **8** ⟨shorthand⟩ ....

54

EVOLUTION DRILLS

In the spaces provided, write the correct shorthand forms.

Brief Forms

1 *progress* ⟋ -s -ing -ed

2 *request* ⟋ -s -ing -ed

3 *satisfy* ⟋ -ing -s -ed

4 *under* ⌒ -go -paid -bid

5 *understand* ⟋ -s -ing -ble

6 *undertake* ⟋ -ing -s -n

7 *state* ⟋ -s -ing -ment

8 *difficult* ⟋ -y -ies

9 *envelope* ⟋ -s *success* ⟋ -s

Phrases

10 *to do* ⟋ -the -that -it

11 *let us* ⟋ -know -see -say

12 *I hope* ⟋ -the -that -this

13 *as soon as* ⟋ -the -this -possible

Recall

14 *consist* ⟋ -s -ing -ed

55

15 demonstrate 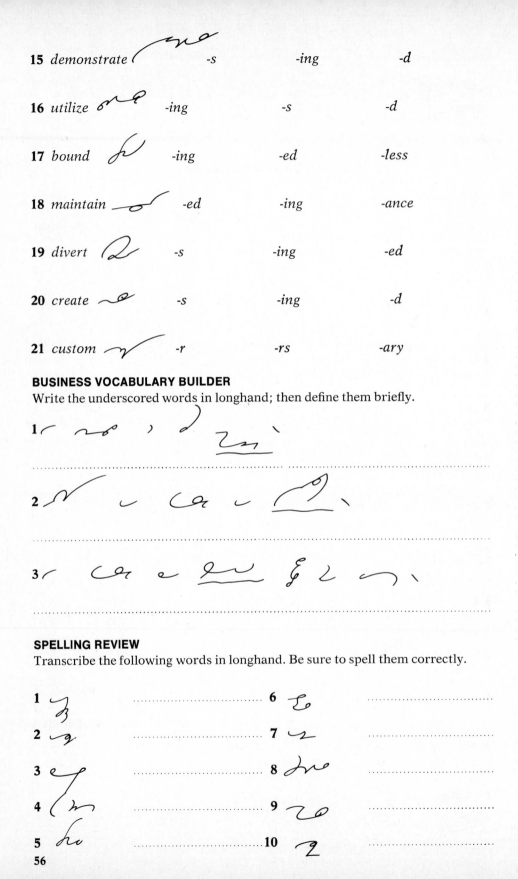 -s   -ing   -d

16 utilize   -ing   -s   -d

17 bound   -ing   -ed   -less

18 maintain   -ed   -ing   -ance

19 divert   -s   -ing   -ed

20 create   -s   -ing   -d

21 custom   -r   -rs   -ary

BUSINESS VOCABULARY BUILDER

Write the underscored words in longhand; then define them briefly.

1 ....

2 ....

3 ....

SPELLING REVIEW

Transcribe the following words in longhand. Be sure to spell them correctly.

1 ....   6 ....

2 ....   7 ....

3 ....   8 ....

4 ....   9 ....

5 ....   10 ....

56

EVOLUTION DRILLS

In the spaces provided, write the correct shorthand forms.

1 dial   -s   -ing   -ed

2 apply   -s   -ing   -ance

3 rely   -s   -ance   -ing

4 comply   -ing   -s   -ance

5 dry   -s   -ing   -r

6 unfair   -ly   unjust   -ly

7 unload   -ing   -s   -ed

8 engrave   -s   -ing   -r

9 enjoy   -s   -ing   -ment

10 diet   -s   -ing   -ed

11 defy   -s   -ing   -ed

12 encourage -s   -ing   -ment

13 engage   -s   -d   -ment

14 <u>uncertain</u>   -paid   -kind   -less

Phrases

15 *we hope* ⟋ -*that* -*the* -*this*

16 *your order* ⟋ -*s* *more than* ⟋ -*the*

17 *of course* ⟋ -*it is* -*it will* -*it will be*

Recall

18 *complain* ⟋ -*s* -*ing* -*ed*

19 *complete* ⟋ -*s* -*ing* -*d*

20 *develop* ⟋ -*s* -*ing* -*ment*

21 *gather* ⟋ -*s* -*ing* -*ed*

22 *appreciate* ⟋ -*s* -*ing* -*d*

23 *custom* ⟋ -*s* -*r* -*rs*

BUSINESS VOCABULARY BUILDER

Write the underscored words in longhand; then define them briefly.

1 ⟋ ⟋ ⟋ . ⟋ ⟋

....

2 ⟋ ⟋ ⟋ , ⟋ ⟋

....

3 ⟋ ⟋ . ⟋ ⟋ . ⟋

....

SPELLING REVIEW

Transcribe the following words in longhand.

1 ⟋ .... 5 ⟋ ....

2 ⟋ .... 6 ⟋ ....

3 ⟋ .... 7 ⟋ ....

4 ⟋ .... 8 ⟋

58

EVOLUTION DRILLS

In the spaces provided, write the correct shorthand forms.

Brief Forms

1 *speak*   -s   -r   -rs

2 *regular*   -ly   *probable*   -ly

3 *newspaper*   -s   *opinion*   -s

4 *particular*   -s   -ly

5 *subject*   -s   -ed   -ive

6 *idea*   -s   *regard*   -ing

Words

7 *long*   -ing   -r   -s

8 *ring*   -s   -ing

9 *king*   -s   -ly   -dom

10 *hang*   -s   -ing   -r

11 *bank*   -s   -r   -rs

12 *drink*   -ing   -r   -s

13 *ink*   -s   -ing   -ed

14 *tank*   -s   -r   -rs

15 *crank* 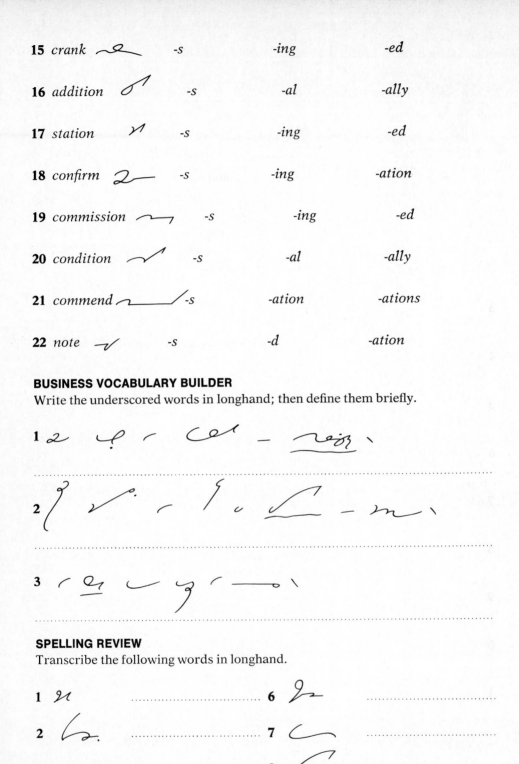	-s	-ing	-ed
16 *addition*	-s	-al	-ally
17 *station*	-s	-ing	-ed
18 *confirm*	-s	-ing	-ation
19 *commission*	-s	-ing	-ed
20 *condition*	-s	-al	-ally
21 *commend*	-s	-ation	-ations
22 *note*	-s	-d	-ation

BUSINESS VOCABULARY BUILDER

Write the underscored words in longhand; then define them briefly.

1 ....

2 ....

3 ....

SPELLING REVIEW

Transcribe the following words in longhand.

1 .... 6 ....

2 .... 7 ....

3 .... 8 ....

4 .... 9 ....

5 ....10 ....

60

EVOLUTION DRILLS

In the spaces provided, write the correct shorthand forms.

1 *await*   -s   -ing   -ed

2 *award*   -s   -ing   -ed

3 *awaken*   -s   -ing   -ed

4 *text*   -s   -book

5 *mix*   -ed   -ing   -s

6 *fix*   -ing   -s   -ed

7 *tax*   -ed   -s   -ing

8 *perplex*   -ing   -ed   -s

9 *brush*   -s   -ing   -ed

10 *second*   -s   -ed   -ary

11 *rush*   -s   -ing   -ed

12 *judge*   -s   -ing   -ment

13 *some*   -thing   -time   -body

14 *touch*   -s   -ing   -ed

15 *bunch* 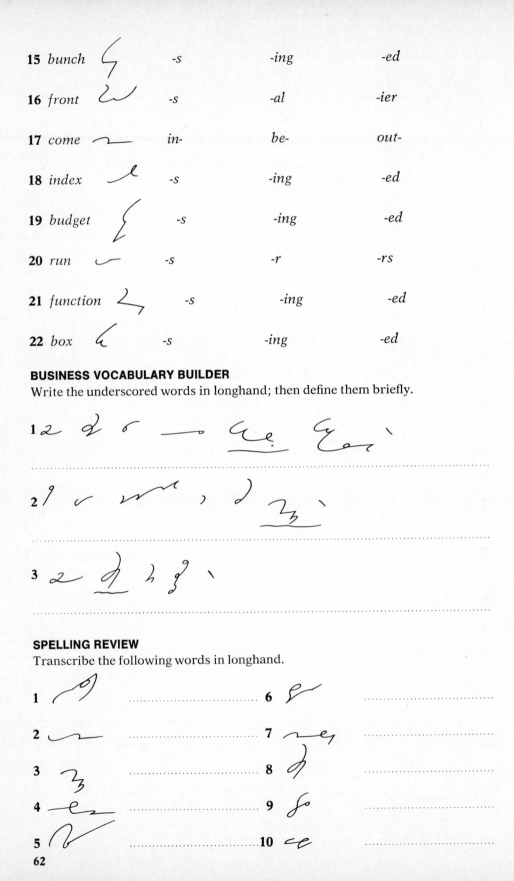	-s	-ing	-ed
16 *front*	-s	-al	-ier
17 *come*	in-	be-	out-
18 *index*	-s	-ing	-ed
19 *budget*	-s	-ing	-ed
20 *run*	-s	-r	-rs
21 *function*	-s	-ing	-ed
22 *box*	-s	-ing	-ed

BUSINESS VOCABULARY BUILDER

Write the underscored words in longhand; then define them briefly.

1

2

3

SPELLING REVIEW

Transcribe the following words in longhand.

1   6

2   7

3   8

4   9

5   10

EVOLUTION DRILLS

In the spaces provided, write the correct shorthand forms.

Brief Forms

1 experience   -s   -d   -ing

2 ordinary   -ly   usual   -ly

3 worth   -y   -less

4 publish   -s   -ed   -ing

5 recognize   -s   -ing   -d

6 world   -ly   public   -ly

Words

7 examine   -s   -ing   -ation

8 exceed   -s   -ing   -ed

9 excite   -s   -d   -ment

10 expert   -s   expense   -s

11 chemical   -s   -ly

12 article   -s   particle   -s

13 surgically   techn-   med-   phys-

14 mechanical   rad-   log-   clin-

15 hope 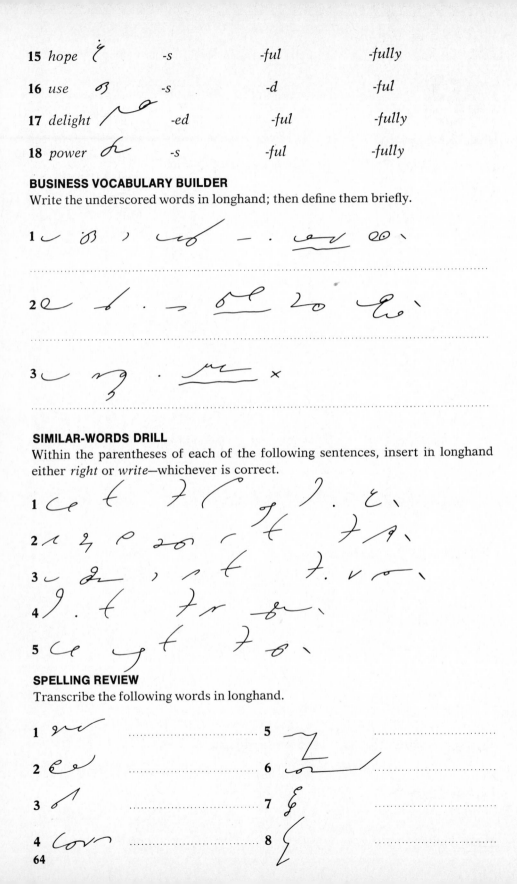	-s	-ful	-fully
16 use	-s	-d	-ful
17 delight	-ed	-ful	-fully
18 power	-s	-ful	-fully

BUSINESS VOCABULARY BUILDER

Write the underscored words in longhand; then define them briefly.

1

....

2

....

3

....

SIMILAR-WORDS DRILL

Within the parentheses of each of the following sentences, insert in longhand either *right* or *write*—whichever is correct.

1

2

3

4

5

SPELLING REVIEW

Transcribe the following words in longhand.

1 .... **5** ....

2 .... **6** ....

3 .... **7** ....

4 .... **8**

EVOLUTION DRILLS

In the spaces provided, write the correct shorthand forms.

Brief Forms

1 *satisfy*　　　　　　-s　　　　　　-ing　　　　　　-ed

2 *publish*　　　　　　-s　　　　　　-ing　　　　　　-ed

3 *regard*　　　　　　-ing　　　　　　-ed　　　　　　-less

4 *speak*　　　　　　-ing　　　　　　-r　　　　　　-rs

5 *newspaper*　　　　-s　　　　*particular*　　　　-ly

6 *state*　　　　　　-s　　　　　　-ment　　　　　　-ments

7 *recognize*　　　　-s　　　　　　-ing　　　　　　-d

8 *wish*　　　　　　-ing　　　　　　-ed　　　　　　-ful

9 *subject*　　　　　-s　　　　　　-ing　　　　　　-ed

10 *opinion*　　　　-s　　　　*ordinary*　　　　-ly

11 *success*　　　　-s　　　　　　-ful　　　　　　-fully

12 *progress*　　　　-s　　　　　　-ing　　　　　　-ive

13 *restate*　　　　-s　　　　　　-ing　　　　　　-d

Phrases

14 *as soon as*　　　-the　　　　　-this　　　　　-possible

15 *we hope* 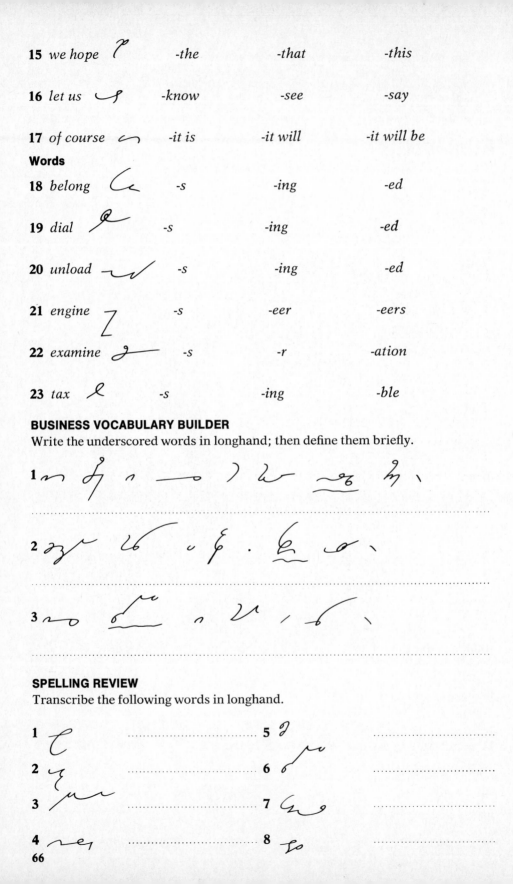   *-the*   *-that*   *-this*

16 *let us*   *-know*   *-see*   *-say*

17 *of course*   *-it is*   *-it will*   *-it will be*

Words

18 *belong*   *-s*   *-ing*   *-ed*

19 *dial*   *-s*   *-ing*   *-ed*

20 *unload*   *-s*   *-ing*   *-ed*

21 *engine*   *-s*   *-eer*   *-eers*

22 *examine*   *-s*   *-r*   *-ation*

23 *tax*   *-s*   *-ing*   *-ble*

BUSINESS VOCABULARY BUILDER

Write the underscored words in longhand; then define them briefly.

1

....

2

....

3

....

SPELLING REVIEW

Transcribe the following words in longhand.

1 ....   **5** ....

2 ....   **6** ....

3 ....   **7** ....

4   **8**

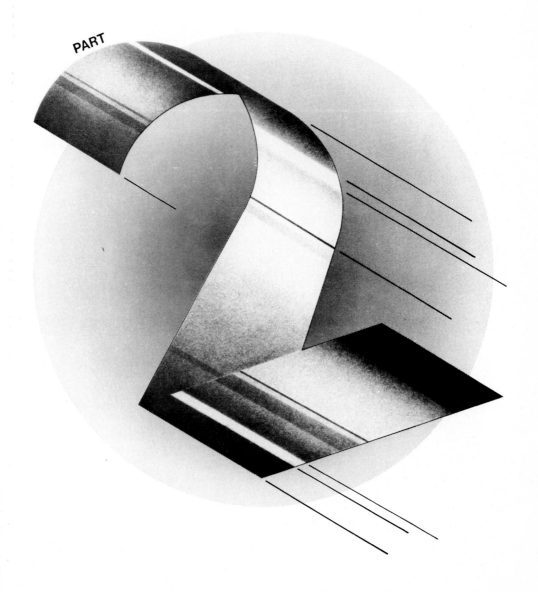

PART

Lessons 31-70

Practice procedures

PUNCTUATION AND SPELLING DRILLS

In Part 2 you will give considerable attention to improving your ability to spell and to punctuate. You will do this through the Spelling and Punctuation Drills, which consist of sentences in shorthand adapted from the Reading and Writing Practice exercises of your textbook. After you have read and copied a Reading and Writing Practice exercise from your textbook, complete the corresponding Punctuation and Spelling Drill in this way:

1 Read an entire sentence aloud. If you cannot immediately read an outline, spell it. If the spelling does not give you the outline, circle it and find out its meaning in class the next day. Do not spend more than a few seconds trying to decipher any outline.

2 Insert the proper punctuation in the shorthand.

3 In the space provided at the right of the page, under "Reason for Punctuation," give the reason for the punctuation you have used. To save time, use the following abbreviations:

1	, parenthetical	, par	**6**	, *when* clause	, when
2	, apposition	, ap	**7**	, *as* clause	, as
3	, series	, ser	**8**	, conjunction	, conj
4	, introductory	, intro	**9**	, *and* omitted	, and o
5	, *if* clause	, if			

A summary of the punctuation rules you will study in *Gregg Shorthand for Colleges, Volume One,* is given in the back of this workbook.

4 Some of the shorthand outlines have small circled numbers above them. Write these words in longhand in the spaces provided at the bottom of the page.

Example

In the workbook you will find:

Reason for Punctuation

The completed drill will look like this:

The word *application* will then be spelled in longhand next to the number 1 under the heading "Spelling Words."

OTHER DRILLS

Suggestions for practicing the other types of drills in Part 2 are given at the point where they are first introduced.

TIME GOALS

Here are some time goals for you to aim for in Part 2:

Lessons 31 through 36	12 minutes
Lessons 37 through 42	10 minutes
Lessons 43 through 48	9 minutes
Lessons 49 through 54	8 minutes
Lessons 55 through 70	7 minutes

If you can complete these lessons in less time, you are making fine progress indeed.

EVOLUTION DRILLS

In the spaces provided, write the correct shorthand forms.

Brief Forms

1 *never*   -theless   *quantity*   -s

2 *object*   -s   -ive   -ed

3 *executive*   -s   *correspond*   -ed

4 *character*   -s   -ize   -ized

5 *govern*   -s   -ing   -ment

Words

6 *picture*   -s   -d   -ing

7 *figure*   -s   -ing   -d

8 *fix*   -s   -ed   -ture

9 *mature*   -s   -ing   -d

10 *nature*   -al   -ally

11 *procedure*   -s   *gradual*   -ly

12 *manual* _____   -s   -ly

13 *schedule*   -s   -ing   -d

14 *equal*   -s   -ing   -ed

PUNCTUATION AND SPELLING

Punctuate the following sentences and write in longhand the spelling words indicated.
Follow the directions on page 69.

[Shorthand outlines for sentences 1–7 appear here, with numbered circles ① through ⑩ marking spelling words and punctuation points.]

Spelling Words

1. .... 6. ....

2. .... 7. ....

3. .... 8. ....

4. .... 9. ....

5. .... 10. ....

72

LESSON 32

EVOLUTION DRILLS

In the spaces provided, write the correct shorthand forms.

1 *haste* ⟍ -ily   *heavy* ⟍ -ily

2 *speed* ⟍ -s   -y   -ily

3 *alter* ⟍ -s   -ed   -ation

4 *disappoint* ⟍ -s   -ment   -ing

5 *discover* ⟍ -s   -ed   -ing

6 *dispose* ⟍ -ing   -s   -d

7 *despair* ⟍ -s   -ing   -ed

8 *describe* ⟍ -ing   -s   -d

9 *temporary* ⟍ -ily   *hearty* ⟍ -ily

10 *dispute* ⟍ -s   -ing   -d

11 *though* ⟍ al-   *together* ⟍ al-

12 *disclose* ⟍ -ing   -s   -d

13 *discourage* ⟍ -s   -d   -ment

14 *steady* ⟍ -ily   *ready* ⟍ -ily

PUNCTUATION AND SPELLING

Punctuate the following sentences and write in longhand the spelling words indicated.
Follow the directions on page 69.

[Shorthand outlines with numbered circles 1–10]

Spelling Words

1		6	
2		7	
3		8	
4		9	
5		10	

74

EVOLUTION DRILLS

In the spaces provided, write the correct shorthand forms.

1 *further*   -s   -ing   -more

2 *force*   -s   -ing   -d

3 *perform*   -s   -ing   -ance

4 *enforce*   -d   -ing   -ment

5 *inform*   -s   -r   -ation

6 *form*   -al   -r   -s

7 *effort*   -s   -less   -lessly

8 *forgive*   -s   -ing   -n

9 *furnish*   -s   -ing   -ed

10 *forecast*   -s   -r   -ing

Phrases

11 *days ago*   months-   minutes-   years- .

12 *few months ago*   -minutes ago

13 *several days ago*   -months ago   -minutes ago

14 *to forget*   -form   -furnish   -force

PUNCTUATION AND SPELLING

Punctuate the following sentences and write in longhand the spelling words indicated.
Follow the directions on page 69.

Reason for Punctuation

[Shorthand outlines for sentences 1–7 with numbered circles 1–10 interspersed]

Spelling Words

1 ....   6 ....

2 ....   7 ....

3 ....   8 ....

4 ....   9 ....

5 ....   10 ....

EVOLUTION DRILLS

In the spaces provided, write the correct shorthand forms.

1 *turn*   -s   -ed   -ing

2 *alternate*   -s   -ing   -d

3 *term*   -s   -ing   -ed

4 *terminate*   -s   -ing   -d

5 *modernize*   -ing   -s   -d

6 *report*   -s   -ed   -r

7 *export*   -s   -ed   -ation

8 *quarter*   -s   -ed   -ly

9 *confirm*   -ing   -s   -ed

10 *inform*   -s   -ation   -ed

11 *exempt*   -s   -ed   -ing

12 *prompt*   -s   -ing   -ed

Phrases

13 I <u>want</u>   you-   they-   who-

14 they <u>wanted</u>   you-   he-   who-

PUNCTUATION AND SPELLING

Punctuate the following sentences and write in longhand the spelling words indicated. Follow the directions on page 69.

[shorthand outlines for sentences 1–7 with numbered circles 1–10]

Spelling Words

1. .... 6. ....

2. .... 7. ....

3. .... 8. ....

4. .... 9. ....

5. .... 10. ....

EVOLUTION DRILLS

In the spaces provided, write the correct shorthand forms.

1 *interest* ⟋ -s -ing -ed

2 *interfere* ⟋ -ing -nce -d

3 *interrupt* ⟋ -ing -s -ed

4 *introduce* ⟋⟍ -s -d -ing

5 *entertain* ⟋ -s -ed -r

6 *enter* ⎯ -s -ing -ed

7 *open* ⟋ -s -ing -ings

8 *build* ⟍ -s -r -ings

9 *clip* ⟍ -s -ing -ings

Phrases

10 <u>*for a long time*</u> ⟍ -minute -moment

11 <u>*one of the*</u> ⟍ -our -them -these

12 <u>*none of our*</u> ⟍ -the -them -these

13 <u>*out of the*</u> ⟍ -this -that -them

14 <u>*some of them*</u> ⟍ -the -these -our

PUNCTUATION AND SPELLING

Punctuate the following sentences and write in longhand the spelling words indicated. Follow the directions on page 69.

Reason for Punctuation

[Shorthand outlines for sentences 1–6 with numbered circles 1–10 and punctuation lines to the right]

Spelling Words

1. ....   6. ....

2. ....   7. ....

3. ....   8. ....

4. ....   9. ....

5. ....   10. ....

RECALL

SIMILAR-WORDS DRILL
Define the following words briefly:

addition ....

edition ....

Within the parentheses of each of the following sentences, write in longhand either *addition* or *edition*—whichever is correct.

1 *[shorthand outlines]*

2 *[shorthand outlines]*

3 *[shorthand outlines]*

4 *[shorthand outlines]*

BUSINESS VOCABULARY BUILDER
Write the underscored words in longhand; then define them briefly.

1 *[shorthand outlines]*

....

2 *[shorthand outlines]*

....

3 *[shorthand outlines]*

....

4 *[shorthand outlines]*

....

5 *[shorthand outlines]*

....

PUNCTUATION AND SPELLING

Punctuate the following sentences and write in longhand the spelling words indicated. Follow the directions on page 69.

Follow the directions on page 69.

Reason for Punctuation

1 [shorthand outline]

2 [shorthand outline]

3 [shorthand outline]

4 [shorthand outline]

5 [shorthand outline]

Spelling Words

1	6	
2	7	
3	8	
4	9	
5	10	

82

EVOLUTION DRILLS

In the spaces provided, write the correct shorthand forms.

1 *increase*   -s   -d   -ingly

2 *exceed*   -s   -ed   -ingly

3 *seem*   -s   -ed   -ingly

4 *approve*   -s   -d   -ingly

5 *import*   -s   -ation   -ing

6 *impress*   -ed   -ing   -ive

7 *impair*   -s   -ed   -ment

8 *embrace*   -d   -s   -ing

9 *embarrass*   -s   -ing   -ment

10 *employ*   -s   -ed   -ing

11 *period*   -ical   -s

12 *situate*   -s   -ing   -d

13 *previous*   -ly   *genuine*   -ly

14 *tedious*   -ly   *courteous*   -ly

PUNCTUATION AND SPELLING

Punctuate the following sentences and write in longhand the spelling words indicated. Follow the directions on page 69.

[Shorthand outlines for sentences 1–8 with numbered punctuation markers]

Spelling Words

1 .... 6 ....

2 .... 7 ....

3 .... 8 ....

4 .... 9 ....

5 .... 10 ....

EVOLUTION DRILLS

In the spaces provided, write the correct shorthand forms.

1 *own* ⌒   -r   -rs   -rship

2 *steam*   -s   -r   -ship

3 *relation*   -s   -ship   -ships

4 *author*   -s   -ize   -ship

5 *town*   -s   -ship   -ships

6 *subscribe*   -s   -r   -ing

7 *subdivide*   -ing   -s   -d

8 *sublease*   -ing   -s   -d

9 *submit*   -s   -ed   -ing

10 *circulate*   -ing   -d   -s

11 *calculate*   -s   -ing   -d

12 *tabulation*   -s   *stipulation*   -s

13 *authority*   -s   *security*   -s

14 *majority*   -s   *minority*   -s

PUNCTUATION AND SPELLING

Punctuate the following sentences and write in longhand the spelling words indicated. Follow the directions on page 69.

Reason for Punctuation

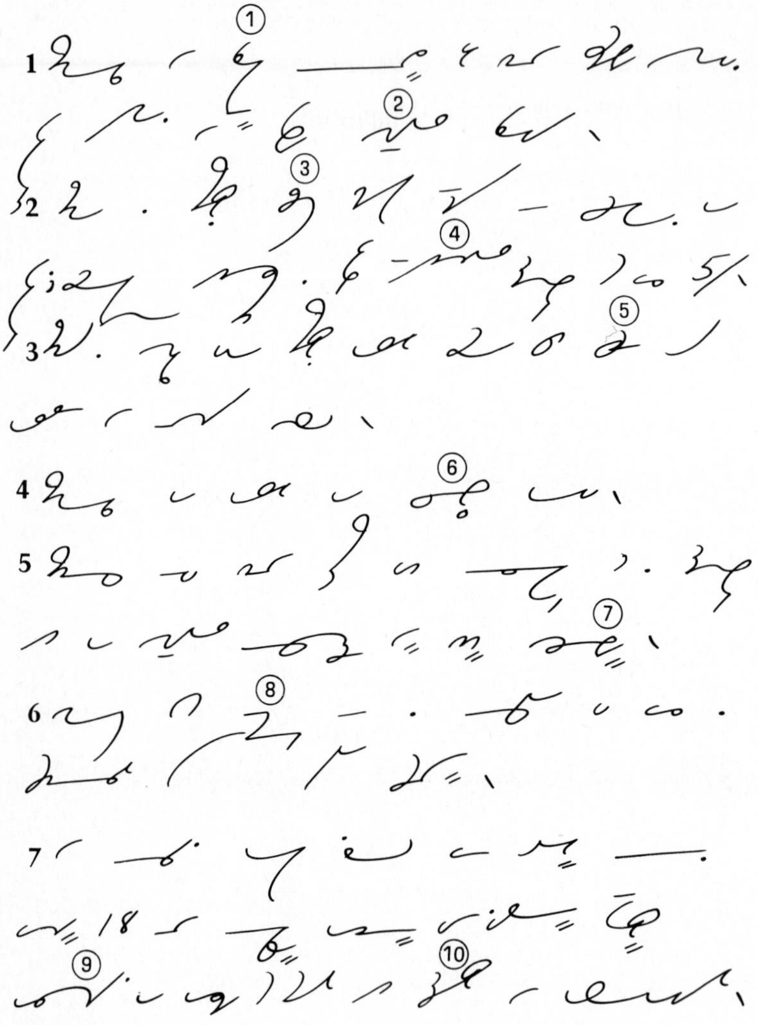

Spelling Words

1	6
2	7
3	8
4	9
5	10

NAME _____ DATE _____

EVOLUTION DRILLS

In the spaces provided, write the correct shorthand forms.

1 *ability* -s   *liability* -s

2 *personality* -s   *locality* -s

3 *facility* -s   *quality* -s

4 *responsibility* -s   *utility* -s

5 *royalty* -s   *casualty* -s

6 *faculty* -s   *penalty* -s

7 *him<u>self</u>* *her-*   *it-*   *my-*

8 *our<u>selves</u>* *your-*   *them-*

Recall

9 *charity* -s   *critical* -ly

10 *partner* -s   -ship   -ships

11 *will* -s   -ing   -ingly

12 *interpret* -s   -r   -ation

13 *import* -s   -r   -ation

14 *submit* -s   -ing   -ed

PUNCTUATION AND SPELLING

Punctuate the following sentences and write in longhand the spelling words indicated. Follow the directions on page 69.

[Shorthand outlines with numbered circles 1–10 appear here, followed by dotted lines for answers in the right margin.]

1 ⟨shorthand⟩ ① ② ....

2 ⟨shorthand⟩ ③ ④ ....

3 ⟨shorthand⟩ ⑤ ....

4 ⟨shorthand⟩ ⑥ ....

5 ⟨shorthand⟩ ....

6 ⟨shorthand⟩ ⑦ ⑧ ....

7 ⟨shorthand⟩ ⑨ ⑩ ....

8 ⟨shorthand⟩ ....

Spelling Words

1 .... 6 ....

2 .... 7 ....

3 .... 8 ....

4 .... 9 ....

5 .... 10 ....

EVOLUTION DRILLS

In the spaces provided, write the correct shorthand forms.

1 *inquire* -s -ing -d

2 *require* -d -ing -ment

3 *contribute* -s -ing -r

4 *attribute* -s -d -ing

5 *substitute* -s *institute* -s

6 *constitute* -s -ing

7 *aptitude* -s *attitude* -s

8 *acquire* -ing -d -s

9 *distribute* -s -d -r

10 *subsequent* -ly *consequent* -ly

Recall

11 *disability* -s *faculty* -s

12 *security* -s *majority* -s

13 *yourself* my- him- her-

14 *subscribe* -s -d -r

PUNCTUATION AND SPELLING

Punctuate the following sentences and write in longhand the spelling words indicated. Follow the directions on page 69.

Reason for Punctuation

[Shorthand outlines for sentences 1–7 with numbered circles 1–10 and punctuation marks, followed by dotted lines for reasons]

Spelling Words

1. ....   6. ....

2. ....   7. ....

3. ....   8. ....

4. ....   9. ....

5. ....   10. ....

90

EVOLUTION DRILLS

In the spaces provided, write the correct shorthand forms.

1 *privilege* 　　　　　　 -s 　　　　　　 -d

2 *inconvenience* 　　　　 -s 　　　　 -ing 　　　　 -d

3 *autograph* 　　　　 -s 　　　　 -ed 　　　　 -ing

4 *photograph* 　　　　 -s 　　　　 -ic 　　　　 -r

5 *transfer* 　　　　 -ed 　　　　 -s 　　　　 -ence

6 *transmit* 　　　　 -s 　　　　 -al 　　　　 -ed

7 *translate* 　　　　 -s 　　　　 -ing 　　　　 -d

8 *transcribe* 　　　　 -s 　　　　 -ing 　　　　 -r

9 *transport* 　　　　 -s 　　　　 -ation 　　　　 -ed

10 *significant* 　　 -ly 　　　　 *anniversary* 　　 -s

11 *memorandum* 　　 -s 　　　　 *reluctant* 　　 -ly

12 *transplant* 　　 -s 　　　　 -ing 　　　　 -ation

13 *statistic* 　　　　 -s 　　　　 -cal 　　　　 -cally

14 *apology* 　　　　 -s 　　　　 -ize 　　　　 -ized

PUNCTUATION AND SPELLING

Punctuate the following sentences and write in longhand the spelling words indicated. Follow the directions on page 69.

[shorthand sentences 1–7 with numbered circles 1–10]

Spelling Words

1 ....   6 ....

2 ....   7 ....

3 ....   8 ....

4 ....   9 ....

5 ....   10 ....

92

RECALL

SIMILAR-WORDS DRILL

Define the following words briefly:

accept ....

except ....

Within the parentheses of each of the following sentences, write in longhand either *accept* or *except*—whichever is correct.

1 ⟋

2

3

4

BUSINESS VOCABULARY BUILDER

Write the underscored words in longhand; then define them briefly.

1

....

2

....

3

....

4

....

5

....

PUNCTUATION AND SPELLING

Punctuate the following sentences and write in longhand the spelling words indicated. Follow the directions on page 69.

[shorthand outlines for sentences 1–6 with numbered circles 1–10]

Spelling Words

1. .... 6. ....

2. .... 7. ....

3. .... 8. ....

4. .... 9. ....

5. .... 10. ....

EVOLUTION DRILLS

In the spaces provided, write the correct shorthand forms.

1 *mistake* _____ -s   -n   -nly

2 *misinform* _____ -s   -ed   -ation

3 *misunderstand* _____ -s   -ing   -ings

4 *supervise* _____ -d   -ing   -r

5 *superintend* _____ -s   -ent   -ents

6 *continue* _____ -s   -ing   -d

7 *communicate* _____ -s   -ing   -d

8 *musical* _____ -s   -ly

9 *mislay* _____ -ed   -ing   -s

10 *misplace* _____ -d   -s   -ing

11 *superior* _____ -s   *superb* _____ -ly

12 *discontinue* _____ -s   -ing   -nce

13 *mutual* _____ -ly   *monument* _____ -s

14 *superhuman* _____ -vision   -sonic   -ficial

95

PUNCTUATION AND SPELLING

Punctuate the following sentences and write in longhand the spelling words indicated. Follow the directions on page 69.

Reason for Punctuation

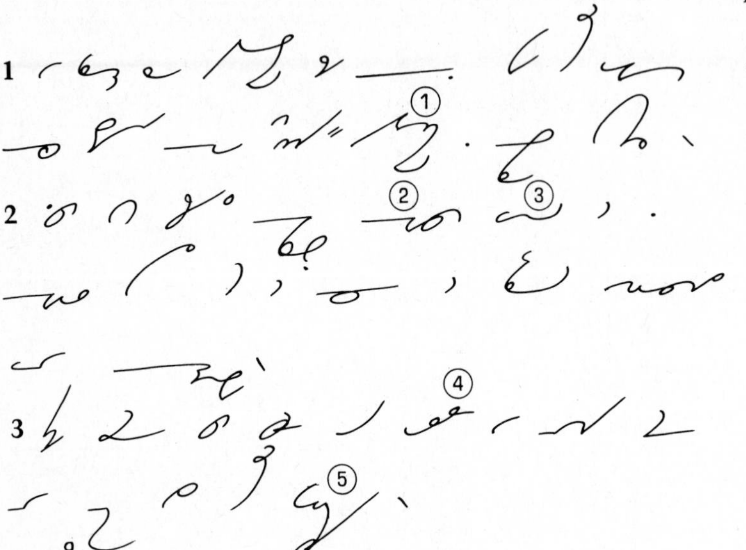

Spelling Words

1 .... 6 ....

2 .... 7 ....

3 .... 8 ....

4 .... 9 ....

5 .... 10 ....

EVOLUTION DRILLS

In the spaces provided, write the correct shorthand forms.

1 _self_-addressed   -defense   -confidence   -reliance

2 _self_-made   -improvement   -supporting   -control

3 circumstance   -s   circumstantial   -ly

4 selfish   -ly   -ness

5 note   -s   -d   -ification

6 class   -s   -ification

7 circumnavigate   -s   -ing   -d

8 circumvent   -s   -ing   -ed

9 specification   -s   qualification   -s

Recall

10 supervise   -ing   -r   -ory

11 miscalculate   -s   -ing   -d

12 continue   -s   -ing   -nce

13 translate   -s   -r   -d

14 autograph   -s   -ed   -ing

97

PUNCTUATION AND SPELLING

Punctuate the following sentences and write in longhand the spelling words indicated. Follow the directions on page 69.

1 [shorthand outline]

2 [shorthand outline]

3 [shorthand outline]

4 [shorthand outline]

5 [shorthand outline]

6 [shorthand outline]

7 [shorthand outline]

8 [shorthand outline]

Spelling Words

1 .... 6 ....

2 .... 7 ....

3 .... 8 ....

4 .... 9 ....

5 .... 10 ....

EVOLUTION DRILLS

In the spaces provided, write the correct shorthand forms.

1 back<u>ward</u>   on-   in-   out-

2 child<u>hood</u>   man-   woman-   boy-

3 awkward   -ly   ultimate   -ly

4 reward   -s   -ing   -ed

5 forward   -ing   -ed   -s

6 result   -s   -ing   -ed

7 consult   -s   -ed   -ing

8 multiply   -ed   -s   -ing

9 adult   -s   insult   -s

Amounts and Quantities

10 600 $600   6,000,000 $6,000,000

11 <u>a</u> dollar   -foot   -pound

12 <u>a</u> hundred   -million   -thousand

13 <u>several</u> hundred   -million   -feet   -pounds

PUNCTUATION AND SPELLING

Punctuate the following sentences and write in longhand the spelling words indicated. Follow the directions on page 69.

[Shorthand outlines with numbered circles 1-10 throughout]

1 *[shorthand]*

2 *[shorthand]*

3 *[shorthand]*

4 *[shorthand]*

5 *[shorthand]*

6 *[shorthand]*

Spelling Words

1.. 6..

2.. 7..

3.. 8..

4.. 9..

5.. 10...

100

EVOLUTION DRILLS

In the spaces provided, write the correct shorthand forms.

1 *program* ⌐   -s   -ing   -ed

2 *diagram* ⌐ tele-   cable-

3 *electric*   -motor   -wire   -fan

4 *electronic*   -s   -ally

5 *electric*   -al   -ally

6 *worth*   -less   -y   -while

7 *anyone*   -how   -where   -body

8 *within*   -stand   -standing   -stood

9 *someone*   -body   -time   -where

Intersection

10 *p.m.*   *a.m.*   *Chamber of Commerce*   *vice versa*

Recall

11 *insult*   -s   -ing   -ed

12 *like*   -s   -d   -lihood

13 *modification*   -s   *specification*   -s

101

PUNCTUATION AND SPELLING

Punctuate the following sentences and write in longhand the spelling words indicated.
Follow the directions on page 69.

[Shorthand outlines for sentences 1–7 with numbered circles 1–10]

Spelling Words

1	6
2	7
3	8
4	9
5	10

EVOLUTION DRILLS

In the spaces provided, write the correct shorthand forms.

1 _Huntington_   Bloom-   Wash-   Lex-

2 _Cunningham_   Buck-   Fram-

3 _Brownsville_   Jackson-   Nash-   Gaines-

4 _Pittsburgh_   Greens-   Harris-   Platts-

Recall

5 _afterward_   up-   on-   out-

6 _neighborhood_   parent-   child-   man-

7 _consult_   -s   -ed   -ation

8 _self-supporting_   -made   -defense   -reliance

9 _accumulate_   -s   -ing   -d

10 _supervise_   -ing   -r   -d

11 _contribute_   -ing   -s   -r

12 _transfer_   -s   -ing   -ence

13 _require_   -d   -ing   -ment

14 _myself_   it-   your-   him-

PUNCTUATION AND SPELLING

Punctuate the following sentences and write in longhand the spelling words indicated. Follow the directions on page 69.

[Shorthand outlines for sentences 1–6 with numbered circles 1–10]

Spelling Words

1		6	
2		7	
3		8	
4		9	
5		10	

104

NAME ______________________________ DATE ______________

LESSON 43

RECALL

SPELLING FAMILIES

Transcribe the following words:

1  ....

2 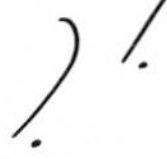 ....

3  ....

4  ....

5  ....

6  ....

SIMILAR-WORDS DRILL

Define the following expressions briefly:

its ....

it's ....

Within the parentheses in each of the following sentences, insert in longhand either *its* or *it's*—whichever is correct.

1 

2 

3 

4 

BUSINESS VOCABULARY BUILDER

Write the underscored words in longhand; then define them briefly.

1 

....

2 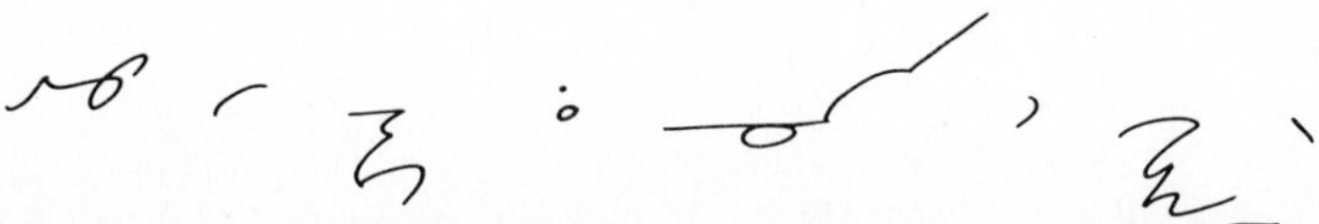

....

PUNCTUATION AND SPELLING

Punctuate the following sentences and write in longhand the spelling words indicated. Follow the directions on page 69.

Follow the directions on page 69.

Reason for Punctuation

[Shorthand outlines for sentences 1–7, with numbered spelling-word indicators (1) through (10)]

Spelling Words

1	6
2	7
3	8
4	9
5	10

EVOLUTION DRILLS

In the spaces provided, write the correct shorthand forms.

1 *wait*   -s   -ing   -r

2 *separate*   -s   -r   -ing

3 *crack*   -s   -ing   -r

4 *map*   -s   -ing   -ed

5 *step*   -ing   -s   -ed

6 *help*   -s   -ed   -r

7 *hit*   -ing   -s   -r

8 *suit*   -s   -ing

9 *give*   -s   -ing   -n

10 *risk*   -s   -ed   -ing

11 *win*   -s   -r   -ing

12 *swim*   -s   -r   -rs

13 *drive*   -s   -r   -rs

14 *arrive*   -s   -ing   -al

15	write		-s		-ing		-r
16	grow		-s		-ing		-n
17	remove		-s		-ing		-d
18	approve		-s		-d		-al
19	increase		-ing		-d		
20	settle		-s		-ing		-rs
21	farm		-s		-r		-rs
22	earn		-s		-r		-rs
23	thick		-er	thin		-ing	
24	throw		-s		-ing		-n

Phrases

25	*I* can		-will		-know		-am
26	*to* go		-get		-tell		-try
27	at *the*		in-		to-		if-
28	*of* these		-the		-our		-my
29	if *you*		-will		-can		-did
30	*we* might		-will		-can		-need

EVOLUTION DRILLS

In the spaces provided, write the correct shorthand forms.

1 *issue*   *ʰ*   -s   -ing   -d

2 *occur* ⌒   -s   -ence   -ed

3 *fold* ⌣   -s   -ing   -r

4 *motion* ⌐ᵧ   -s   -ing   -ed

5 *promise* ⌐ₚ   -ing   -d   -s

6 *cause* ⌐ᵧ   -d   -ing   -s

7 *notice* ⌐ₑ   -ing   -d   -s

8 *retire* ⌐ₑ   -s   -ing   -d

9 *act* ⌐ᵥ   -s   -ing   -ive

10 *caution* ⌐ᵧ   -s   -ing   -ed

11 *prepare* ⌐   -s   -ing   -d

12 *believe* ⌐   -s   -ing   -d

13 *paint* ⌐   -s   -ing   -r

14 *hold* ⌐   -s   -ing   -r

15 *reach*   ✓   -s   -ing   -ed

16 *hire*   ∂   -s   -ing   -d

17 *rent*   ∽   -s   -ed   -al

18 *efficient*   ℓ   -ly   *proficient*   ℓ   -ly

19 *pressure*   ℓℎ   -s   -ing   -d

20 *brief*   ℓ   -s   -r   -ly

21 *oblige*   ℓℊ   -s   -ing   -d

22 *call*   ∽   -ing   -s   -ed

23 *fair*   ∂   -ness   -r   -ly

Phrases

24 *to pay*   6   -please   -plan   -place

25 *from which*   ⤵   -that   -the   -them

26 *he should*   ✓   I-   you-   we-

27 *they may*   ⟲   -can   -will   -are

28 *for the*   ∠   -this   -them

29 *have been*   )   you-   we-   I-

30 *to be able*   ⌐   should-   will-   would-

110

EVOLUTION DRILLS

In the spaces provided, write the correct shorthand forms.

1 *accept*   -s   -ed   -ble

2 *book*   -s   -ing   -let

3 *cover*   -s   -ed   -ing

4 *persuade*   -s   -ing   -d

5 *permit*   -s   -ing   -ed

6 *purchase*   -d   -r   -rs

7 *design*   -s   -r   -ed

8 *depend*   -s   -ing   -ed

9 *direct*   -s   -ed   -ing

10 *need*   -s   -ing   -ed

11 *hunt*   -s   -ing   -r

12 *list*   -ed   -ing   -less

13 *noise*   -s   -y   -less

14 *fill*   -ing   -ed   -s

111

15 *quote* ⤳   -ing   -s   -d

16 *yell* ⤳   -s   *yard* ⤳   -s

17 *refer* ⤳   -s   -ed   -ence

18 *boil* ⤳   -s   -r   -ed

19 *amend* ⤳ -s   -ing   -ed

20 *eliminate* ⤳ -s   -ing   -d

21 *audit* ⤳   -s   -r   -rs

22 *grade* ⤳   -s   -ing   -d

23 *person* ⤳   -s   -al   -ally

Phrases

24 <u>we may</u> ⤳   -should   -will   -are

25 *who* <u>can</u> ⤳   we-   he-   you-

26 *they* <u>think</u> ⤳   we-   you-   who-

27 <u>about</u> *you* ⤳   -it   -that   -these

BUSINESS VOCABULARY BUILDER

Write the underscored words in longhand; then define them briefly.

1 ⤳ <u>⤳</u> ⤳ ⤳ ⤳

....

2 ⤳ ⤳ <u>⤳</u> ⤳ ⤳

....

EVOLUTION DRILLS

In the spaces provided, write the correct shorthand forms.

1 *refuse*   -s   -ing   -al

2 *appreciate* -s   -ing   -d

3 *establish*   -s   -ed   -ment

4 *element*   -s   -al   -ary

5 *initial*   -s   -ing   -ed

6 *count*   -ed   -r   -less

7 *bother*   -s   -ing   -ed

8 *consider*   -s   -ate   -ble

9 *obtain*   -s   -ing   -ed

10 *tend*   -s   -ing   -ed

11 *accident*   -s   -al   -ally

12 *difference* -s   *divide*   -s

13 *compare*   -s   -ing   -d

14 *attempt*   -ing   -ed   -s

113

15 develop ⟍ -ment   defeat ⟍ -ed

16 demonstrate ⟋ -s   -ing

Phrases

17 <u>to me</u> ⟋ -make   -know

18 that <u>time</u> ⟋ on-   in-   this-

19 <u>over</u> that ⟋ -this   -them   -these

20 <u>several</u> days ⟋ -months   -minutes   -times

21 Wednesday <u>morning</u> ⟋ Tuesday-   Thursday-

SPELLING FAMILIES

Add either *-ment* or *-ement* to the following word beginnings to obtain the correct spelling of each word.

argu *ment* ....judg .... manag ....

amus ....requir .... stat ....

engag ....acknowledg .... arrang ....

advertis ....announc .... encourag ....

BUSINESS VOCABULARY BUILDER

Write the underscored expressions in longhand; then define them briefly.

1 ⟋ shorthand outline

....

2 ⟋ shorthand outline

....

3 ⟋ shorthand outline

....

114

EVOLUTION DRILLS

In the spaces provided, write the correct shorthand forms.

1 *examine* _____ -s   -ing   -ation

2 *explain* _____ -s   -ed   -ing

3 *await* _____ -s   -ed   -ing

4 *chemical* _____ -s   *critical* _____ -ly

5 *box* _____ -s   -ed   -ing

6 *refund* _____ -s   -ing   -ed

7 *help* _____ -s   -ful   -fully

8 *long* _____ -s   -r   -ing

9 *tank* _____ -s   -r   -rs

10 *confirm* _____ -s   -ing   -ation

11 *unload* _____ -s   -ing   -ed

12 *encourage* _____ -s   -d   -ment

13 *comply* _____ -s   -ed   -ance

14 *appreciate* _____ -s   -ing   -d

Phrases

15 *of course* ⌢ -*it is* -*it will* -*it will be*

16 *let us* ⌣⌐ -*know* -*see* -*say*

17 *to do* ╱ -*the* -*that* -*this*

18 *as soon as* ♀ -*the* -*this* -*possible*

19 *we hope* ℓ -*you will* -*you will be* -*you will not be*

20 *I hope* ℓ -*you will* -*you will be* -*you will not be*

21 *on this* ⌐⌐ -*that* -*them* -*our*

SPELLING REVIEW
Transcribe the following words in longhand:

1 ....   5 ....

2 ....   6 ....

3 ....   7 ....

4 ....   8 ....

BUSINESS VOCABULARY BUILDER
Write the underscored words in longhand; then define them briefly.

1 ....

....

2 ....

....

3 ....

....

116

EVOLUTION DRILLS

In the spaces provided, write the correct shorthand forms.

1 *lecture* _____ -s   -ing   -r

2 *determine* _____ -s   -ing   -ation

3 *inform* _____ -s   -ed   -ation

4 *interfere* _____ -s   -ence   -d

5 *furnish* _____ -ing   -ings   -ed

SIMILAR-WORDS DRILL

Within the parentheses in each of the following sentences, insert in longhand *their*, *there*, or *they're*—whichever is correct.

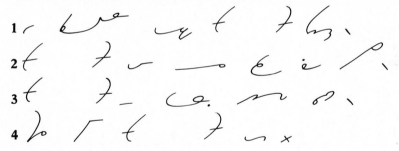

BUSINESS VOCABULARY BUILDER

Write the underscored words in longhand; then define them briefly.

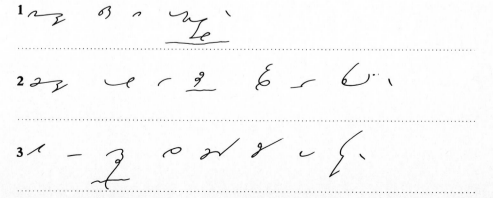

PUNCTUATION AND SPELLING

Punctuate the following sentences and write in longhand the spelling words indicated. Follow the directions on page 69.

Reason for Punctuation

1

2

3

4

5

6

Spelling Words

1 .... 6 ....

2 .... 7 ....

3 .... 8 ....

4 .... 9 ....

5 .... 10 ....

EVOLUTION DRILLS

In the spaces provided, write the correct shorthand forms.

1 *embarrass*   -ing   -ed   -ment

2 *myself*   *your-*   *him-*   *her-*

3 *exceed*   -s   -ed   -ingly

4 *submit*   -s   -ing   -ed

5 *transcribe*   -s   -ing   -r

GRAMMAR CHECKUP

The following sentences contain split infinitives. Indicate, as in the example below, where the word "splitting" the infinitive should be transferred to make the sentence read smoothly.

Example:

1

2

3

BUSINESS VOCABULARY BUILDER

Write the underscored words in longhand; then define them briefly.

1

....

2

....

3

....

119

PUNCTUATION AND SPELLING

Punctuate the following sentences and write in longhand the spelling words indicated. Follow the directions on page 69.

Reason for Punctuation

[Shorthand notation — sentences 1 through 6 with circled numbers 1–10]

Spelling Words

1. .... 6. ....

2. .... 7. ....

3. .... 8. ....

4. .... 9. ....

5. .... 10. ....

120

EVOLUTION DRILLS

In the spaces provided, write the correct shorthand forms.

1 *program*   -s   -ed   -ing

2 *neighbor<u>hood</u>*   *child-*   *parent-*   *woman-*

3 *<u>self</u>-made*   *-defense*   *-confidence*   *-improvement*

4 *supervise*   -s   -r   -ing

5 *forward*   -ing   -ed   -s

6 *multiply*   -ing   -s   -ed

7 *electric*   -al   *electronic*   -s

COMMON PREFIXES

Super- means ....

Define the following words briefly:

supervise ....

superior ....

superfluous ....

BUSINESS VOCABULARY BUILDER

Write the underscored words in longhand; then define them briefly.

1

....

2

....

PUNCTUATION AND SPELLING

Punctuate the following sentences and write in longhand the spelling words indicated. Follow the directions on page 69.

Reason for Punctuation

Spelling Words

1 .... 6 ....

2 .... 7 ....

3 .... 8 ....

4 .... 9 ....

5 .... 10 ....

EVOLUTION DRILLS
In the spaces provided, write the correct shorthand forms.

1 *govern*   -r   -ment   -ments

2 *suggest*   -s   -ing   -tion

3 *advertise*   -d   -ing   -ment

4 *manufacture*   -s   -r   -rs

5 *present*   -s   -ing   -ation

SPELLING FAMILIES
Add either *-tion* or *-sion* to the following word beginnings to obtain the correct spelling of each word.

conclu .... *informa* .... *profes* ....

applica .... *organiza* .... *ques* ....

deci .... *occa* .... *selec* ....

BUSINESS VOCABULARY BUILDER
Write the underscored words in longhand; then define them briefly.

1
....

2
....

3
....

PUNCTUATION AND SPELLING

Punctuate the following sentences and write in longhand the spelling words indicated. Follow the directions on page 69.

[Shorthand outlines for sentences 1–6 with numbered spelling word indicators 1–10]

Spelling Words

1 ....   6 ....

2 ....   7 ....

3 ....   8 ....

4 ....   9 ....

5 ....   10 ....

124

EVOLUTION DRILLS

In the spaces provided, write the correct shorthand forms.

1 <u>some of these</u> ⟋⟍ -the   -them   -our

2 <u>let us</u> ⟍ᵖ -see   -know   -say

3 weeks <u>ago</u> ⟋⟍ days-   years-   months-

4 I <u>wanted</u> ⟋ he-   you-   who-

5 <u>none of the</u> ⟍ -these   -them   -our

GRAMMAR CHECKUP

Underscore the expression or word that is not in parallel construction in the following sentences. Indicate in the space provided the expression you would use to make each sentence parallel.

Example: ⟋ ⟍ ⟋ ⟍ ⟍ _ _ *interesting*

1 ⟍ ⟋ ⟍ ⟍ ⟍ ⟍ ....
⟍ ⟍ ....

2 ⟍ ⟋ ⟍ ⟍ ⟍ ....

BUSINESS VOCABULARY BUILDER

Write the underscored words in longhand; then define them briefly.

1 ⟋ <u>⟍</u> ⟍ ⟍ ⟍
....

2 ⟍ ⟍ ⟍ ⟍
....

PUNCTUATION AND SPELLING

Punctuate the following sentences and write in longhand the spelling words indicated. Follow the directions on page 69.

Reason for Punctuation

1 [shorthand outlines]

2 [shorthand outlines]

3 [shorthand outlines]

4 [shorthand outlines]

5 [shorthand outlines]

6 [shorthand outlines]

Spelling Words

1 .... 6 ....

2 .... 7 ....

3 .... 8 ....

4 .... 9 ....

5 .... 10 ....

EVOLUTION DRILLS
In the spaces provided, write the correct shorthand forms.

1 *become*   -s   -ing   -ingly

2 *condense*   -d   -ing   -ation

3 *complete*   -s   -d   -ly

4 *explain*   -s   -ed   -ation

5 *deserve*   -s   -ing   -d

6 *mistake*   -s   -n   -nly

7 *replace*   -d   -ing   -ment

SPELLING FAMILIES
Add either *-ible* or *-able* to the following word beginnings to complete each word correctly.

avail .... *suit* .... *consider* ....

sens .... *respons* .... *reason* ....

cap .... *incred* .... *flex* ....

BUSINESS VOCABULARY BUILDER
Write the underscored words in longhand; then define them briefly.

1 _____

2 _____

PUNCTUATION AND SPELLING

Punctuate the following sentences and write in longhand the spelling words indicated. Follow the directions on page 69.

Reason for Punctuation

(shorthand outlines with numbered markers 1–10)

1 ....

2 ....

....

....

....

....

....

....

....

....

....

Spelling Words

1............................	6............................
2............................	7............................
3............................	8............................
4............................	9............................
5............................	10...........................

EVOLUTION DRILLS

In the spaces provided, write the correct shorthand forms.

1 *cable*    *-s*   *-d*   *-ing*

2 *invest<u>ment</u>*   *adjust-*   *require-*   *amuse-*

3 *equal*   *-ized*   *-ize*   *-ly*

4 *hope*   *-d*   *-ful*   *-fully*

5 *mention*   *-s*   *-ing*   *-ed*

6 *initial*   *-s*   *-ed*   *-ing*

7 *steady*   *-ily*   *ready*   *-ily*

COMMON PREFIXES

Pre- means ....

Define the following words briefly:

predict ....

precaution ....

preliminary ....

BUSINESS VOCABULARY BUILDER

Write the underscored words in longhand; then define them briefly.

1

....

2

....

129

PUNCTUATION AND SPELLING

Punctuate the following sentences and write in longhand the spelling words indicated. Follow the directions on page 69.

[Shorthand outlines for sentences 1–7, with numbered circles 1–10 indicating spelling words]

Spelling Words

1 .... 6 ....

2 .... 7 ....

3 .... 8 ....

4 .... 9 ....

5 .... 10 ....

130

EVOLUTION DRILLS

In the spaces provided, write the correct shorthand forms.

1 *entertain* -s -ing -ment

2 <u>*undergo*</u> -take -stand -ground

3 <u>*overcome*</u> -do -tired -paid

4 *introduce* -ing -d -s

5 <u>*electric*</u> *light* -fan -motor -razor

6 *interest* -ed -ing -ingly

7 *enter* -s -ed -ing

8 *transport* -ed -ing -ation

9 *supervise* -d -r -ing

10 <u>*self-*</u> -assurance -confidence -determination
   reliant

11 *circumstance* -s *circumvent* -s

GRAMMAR CHECKUP

Each of the following sentences contains a comparative form that is used incorrectly. Underscore the incorrect comparative, and write the correct form in the space provided.

Example: ....*more*............

1 ....

2 ....

3 ....

4 ....

131

PUNCTUATION AND SPELLING

Punctuate the following sentences and write in longhand the spelling words indicated. Follow the directions on page 69.

[Shorthand outlines for sentences 1–7, with numbered circles 1–10 indicating spelling words, and dotted lines in the right margin for punctuation reasons.]

Spelling Words

1 .... 6 ....

2 .... 7 ....

3 .... 8 ....

4 .... 9 ....

5 .... 10 ....

132

EVOLUTION DRILLS

In the spaces provided, write the correct shorthand forms.

1 *stipulate*   -s   -ing   -ation

2 *minority* _____ -s   *majority*   -s

3 *chemical*   -s   -ly

4 *monogram* _____ pro-   radio-   cable-

5 *sparingly*   will-   know-   grudge-

6 *upward*   in-   out-   for-

7 *parenthood*   neighbor-   child-   woman-

SIMILAR-WORDS DRILL

Within the parentheses of the following sentences, insert either *county* or *country*—whichever is correct.

1

2

3

BUSINESS VOCABULARY BUILDER

Write the underscored words in longhand; then define them briefly.

1

....

2

....

PUNCTUATION AND SPELLING

Punctuate the following sentences and write in longhand the spelling words indicated. Follow the directions on page 69.

Follow the directions on page 69.

Reason for Punctuation

1

2

3

4

5

6

Spelling Words

1 .... 6 ....

2 .... 7 ....

3 .... 8 ....

4 .... 9 ....

5 .... 10 ....

134

EVOLUTION DRILLS

In the spaces provided, write the correct shorthand forms.

1 *land* 　*-ed*　　　　*-ing*　　　　*-ings*

2 *plant*　　　*-s*　　　　*-ing*　　　　*-r*

3 *friend*　　　*-s*　　　　*-ly*　　　　*-liness*

4 *differ*　　　*-s*　　　　*-ent*　　　　*-ence*

5 *examine*　　　*-s*　　　　*-r*　　　　*-ation*

6 *condemn*　　　*-s*　　　　*-ing*　　　　*-ed*

7 *deduct*　　　*-s*　　　　*-ing*　　　　*-ed*

COMMON PREFIXES

Pro- means ....

Define the following words briefly:

proceed ....

program ....

produce ....

BUSINESS VOCABULARY BUILDER

Write the underscored words in longhand; then define them briefly.

1 ....

2 ....

PUNCTUATION AND SPELLING

Punctuate the following sentences and write in longhand the spelling words indicated. Follow the directions on page 69.

Reason for Punctuation

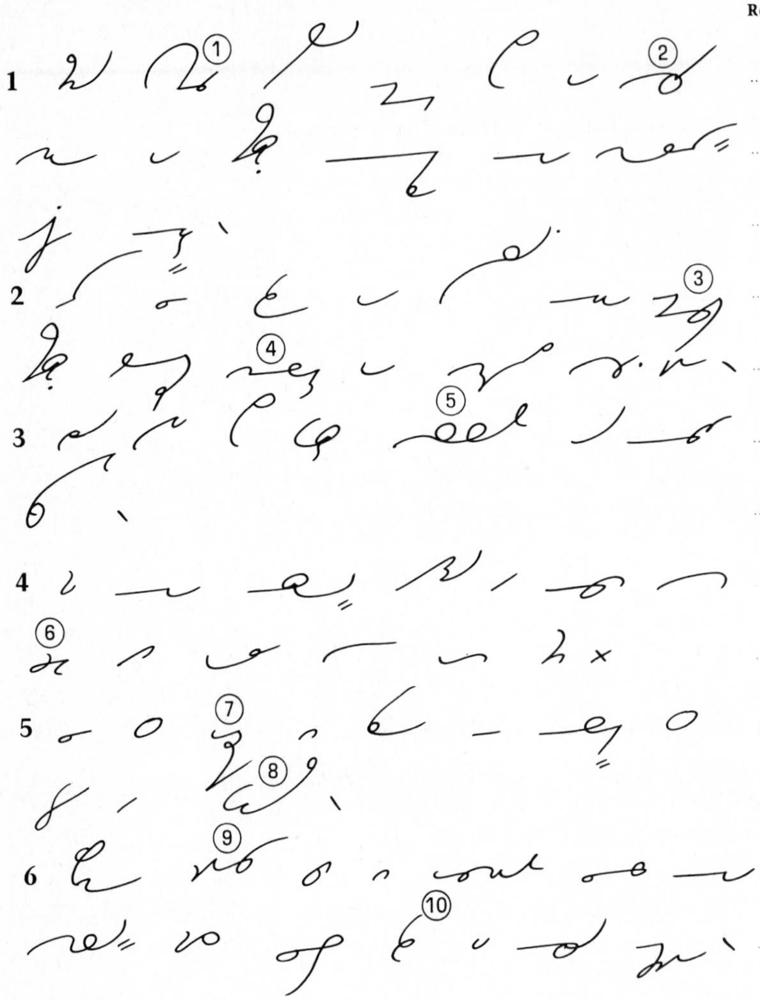

Spelling Words

1 .... 6 ....

2 .... 7 ....

3 .... 8 ....

4 .... 9 ....

5 .... 10 ....

EVOLUTION DRILLS

In the spaces provided, write the correct shorthand forms.

1 *read<u>er</u>*   *lead-*   *near-*   *dear-*

2 *serious*   *-ly*   *obvious*   *-ly*

3 *continue*   *-s*   *-ing*   *-d*

4 *condition*   *-s*   *-al*   *-ally*

5 *smudge*   *-s*   *-d*   *-ing*

SPELLING FAMILIES

Add either *-ious* or *-eous* to the following word beginnings to complete each word correctly.

ser .... *simultan* .... *var* ....

ted .... *advantag* .... *erron* ....

court .... *grac* .... *spontan* ....

BUSINESS VOCABULARY BUILDER

Write the underscored words in longhand; then define them briefly.

1

....

2

....

3

....

PUNCTUATION AND SPELLING

Punctuate the following sentences and write in longhand the spelling words indicated. Follow the directions on page 69.

Reason for Punctuation

[Shorthand outlines with numbered punctuation markers 1–10]

1 ....

2 ....

3 ....

4 ....

5 ....

6 ....

7 ....

8 ....

9 ....

10 ....

Spelling Words

1 ....   6 ....

2 ....   7 ....

3 ....   8 ....

4 ....   9 ....

5 ....   10 ....

EVOLUTION DRILLS

In the spaces provided, write the correct shorthand forms.

1 *speak*   -s   -r   -rs

2 *progress*   -s   -ed   -ive

3 *state*   -s   -ment   -ments

4 *worth*   -y   -less   -while

5 *recognize*   -ing   -s   -d

6 *regard*   -s   -less   -ed

7 *request*   -s   -ed   -ing

SIMILAR-WORDS DRILL

Within the parentheses in each of the following sentences, write in longhand either *ad* or *add*—whichever is correct.

1

2

3

BUSINESS VOCABULARY BUILDER

Write the underscored words in longhand; then define them briefly.

1

....

2

....

PUNCTUATION AND SPELLING

Punctuate the following sentences and write in longhand the spelling words indicated. Follow the directions on page 69.

Follow the directions on page 69.

Reason for Punctuation

[Shorthand outlines for sentences 1–6, with numbered circles 1–10 marking spelling words and punctuation points]

Spelling Words

1 ....   6 ....

2 ....   7 ....

3 ....   8 ....

4 ....   9 ....

5 ....   10 ....

140

EVOLUTION DRILLS

In the spaces provided, write the correct shorthand forms.

1 *work* ⌒   -s   -ing   -ed

2 *advantage*   -s   -ous   -ously

3 *business*   -like   -man   -woman

4 *object*   -s   -ed   -ive

5 *experience*   -s   -d   -ing

6 *manufacture*   -s   -r   -rs

COMMON PREFIXES

Un- means ....

Define the following words briefly:

uncommon ....

uncertain ....

unsolicited ....

unsatisfactory ....

BUSINESS VOCABULARY BUILDER

Write the underscored words in longhand; then define them briefly.

1 ....

2 ....

PUNCTUATION AND SPELLING

Punctuate the following sentences and write in longhand the spelling words indicated. Follow the directions on page 69.

Follow the directions on page 69.

Reason for Punctuation

Spelling Words

1		6	
2		7	
3		8	
4		9	
5		10	

142

EVOLUTION DRILLS

In the spaces provided, write the correct shorthand forms.

1 *we hope*   〸   *-the*   *-that*   *-you*

2 *let us*   〰   *-make*   *-know*   *-have*

3 *some of the*   〰   *-our*   *-them*   *-these*

4 *as soon as*   〰   *-you*   *-the*   *-possible*

5 *have been able*   〰   *we-*   *you-*   *who-*

6 *be sure*   〰   *to-*   *can-*   *may-*

GRAMMAR CHECKUP

One of the expressions in parentheses in each of the following sentences is correct. Underscore that word and transcribe it in longhand in the space provided.

1 ....

2 ....

3 ....

4 ....

BUSINESS VOCABULARY BUILDER

Write the underscored words in longhand; then define them briefly.

1 ....

....

2 ....

....

PUNCTUATION AND SPELLING

Punctuate the following sentences and write in longhand the spelling words indicated. Follow the directions on page 69.

Reason for Punctuation

1
2
3
4
5
6
7

Spelling Words

1
2
3
4
5
6
7
8
9
10

EVOLUTION DRILLS

In the spaces provided, write the correct shorthand forms.

1 *export* ℰ   -s   -ed   -ation

2 *complete*   -s   -d .   -ly

3 *consult*   -s   -ing   -ation

4 *misplace*   -d   -s   -ing

5 *depart*   -s   -ed   -ment

SIMILAR-WORDS DRILL

Within the parentheses in each of the following sentences, write in longhand *loss, lose,* or *loose*—whichever is correct.

1

2

3

4

BUSINESS VOCABULARY BUILDER

Write the underscored words in longhand; then define them briefly.

1

....

2

....

3

....

145

PUNCTUATION AND SPELLING

Punctuate the following sentences and write in longhand the spelling words indicated. Follow the directions on page 69.

Reason for Punctuation

Spelling Words

1 ....
6 ....

2 ....
7 ....

3 ....
8 ....

4 ....
9 ....

5 ....
10 ....

EVOLUTION DRILLS

In the spaces provided, write the correct shorthand forms.

1 *report*   -ed   -ing   -r

2 *ourselves*   them-   your-

3 *efficient*   -ly   *proficient*   -ly

4 *believe*   -s   -ing   -d

5 *compliment*   -s   -ary   -ing

6 *trouble*   -s   -d   -ing

COMMON PREFIXES

Trans- means ....

Define the following words briefly:

transfer ....

transport ....

transmit ....

transcontinental ....

BUSINESS VOCABULARY BUILDER

Write the underscored words in longhand; then define them briefly.

1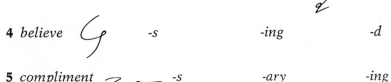

....

2

....

PUNCTUATION AND SPELLING

Punctuate the following sentences and write in longhand the spelling words indicated. Follow the directions on page 69.

1 *[shorthand outlines]*

2 *[shorthand outlines]*

3 *[shorthand outlines]*

4 *[shorthand outlines]*

5 *[shorthand outlines]*

6 *[shorthand outlines]*

Spelling Words

1	6
2	7
3	8
4	9
5	10

148

EVOLUTION DRILLS

In the spaces provided, write the correct shorthand forms.

1 *engage*   -s   -d   -ment

2 *inform*   -s   -ed   -ing

3 *invest*   -s   -ed   -ment

4 *commit*   -s   -ed   -ing

5 *employ*   -s   -ed   -ment

6 *confer*   -s   -ed   -ence

7 *reject*   -s   -ed   -ing

8 *discourage*   -s   -d   -ment

SPELLING FAMILIES

Transcribe the following words, each of which has an ending of -er, or, or -ar.

1 ....   8 ....

2 ....   9 ....

3 ....   10 ....

4 ....   11 ....

5 ....   12 ....

6 ....   13 ....

7 ....   14 ....

PUNCTUATION AND SPELLING

Punctuate the following sentences and write in longhand the spelling words indicated. Follow the directions on page 69.

1 _[shorthand outlines]_

2 _[shorthand outlines]_

3 _[shorthand outlines]_

4 _[shorthand outlines]_

5 _[shorthand outlines]_

Spelling Words

1 .... 6 ....

2 .... 7 ....

3 .... 8 ....

4 .... 9 ....

5 .... 10 ....

Appendix
Summary of Punctuation Rules

Summary of Punctuation Rules

, parenthetical

In order to make his meaning clearer, a writer sometimes inserts a comment or an explanation that could be omitted without changing the meaning of the sentence. These added comments and explanations are called *parenthetical* and are separated from the rest of the sentence by commas.

If the parenthetical word or expression occurs at the beginning or end of a sentence, only one comma is needed.

I feel, therefore, that we should change our plans.

Don't you think, Mr. Smith, that the price is too high?

We will send you a copy, of course.

, apposition

Sometimes a writer mentions a person or thing and then, in order to make the meaning perfectly clear to the reader, says the same thing again in different words.

My neighbor, Mr. Harry Green, owns a sailboat.

The meeting will be held on Friday, April 16, at the Hotel Brown.

In many cases these constructions in apposition resemble the constructions in which the commas are used to set off parenthetical expressions. It is really immaterial whether the transcribers think they are using the commas to set off an appositive or to set off a parenthetical expression, for the results are identical.

An expression in apposition is set off by two commas, except at the end of a sentence, when only one comma is necessary.

Meet my neighbor, Harry Green.

, series

When the last member of a series of three or more items is preceded by *and* or *or*, place a comma before the conjunction, as well as between the other items.

I bought a tie, a coat, and a pair of shoes.

I talked to him on July 1, on July 3, and on July 18.

Her duties consisted of receiving callers, answering the telephone, and opening the mail.

, *if* clause

One of the most frequent errors made by the beginning transcriber is the failure to make a complete sentence. In most cases the incomplete sentence is a dependent or subordinate clause introduced by *as, when,* or *if.* The dependent or subordinate clause deceives the transcriber because it is a complete sentence except that it is introduced by a word such as *if;* therefore, it requires another clause to complete the thought.

The dependent or subordinate clause *often* signals the coming of the main clause by means of a subordinate conjunction. The commonest subordinating conjunctions are *if, as,* and *when.* Other subordinating conjunctions are *though, although, whether, unless, because, since, while, where, after, whenever, until, before,* and *now.*

A subordinate clause introduced by *if* and followed by the main clause is separated from the main clause by a comma.

If you cannot be present, please notify me.

If you finish before noon, you are free to go home.

, *as* clause

A subordinate clause introduced by *as* and followed by the main clause is separated from the main clause by a comma.

As I am sure you are aware, the store closes at five.

As I told you on the telephone, I cannot preside at the meeting.

, *when* clause

A subordinate clause introduced by *when* and followed by the main clause is separated from the main clause by a comma.

When you finish the job, please let me know.

When John arrives, ask him to see me.

, introductory

A comma is used to separate the subordinate clause from a following main clause. You have already studied the application of this rule to subordinate clauses introduced by *if, as,* and *when.* Here are additional examples:

While I understand the statement, I do not agree with it.

Although it was only 3 o'clock, he closed the office.

Before you let out your next advertising contract, give us an opportunity to discuss it with you.

A comma is also used after introductory words or phrases such as *furthermore, on the contrary,* and *for instance.*

Furthermore, you made a mistake in grammar.

On the contrary, you are at fault.

For your convenience in sending me the information I need, I am enclosing a stamped envelope.

▶ Note: If the subordinate clause or other introductory expression follows the main clause, the comma is usually not necessary.

I am enclosing a stamped envelope for your convenience in sending me the information I need.

, conjunction

A comma is used to separate two independent clauses that are joined by one of the following conjunctions: *and, but, or, for, nor.*

An independent clause (sometimes called a main or a principal clause) is one that has a subject and predicate and that could stand alone as a complete sentence.

The unit is one of the most dependable on the market, and it is economical to operate.

The first independent clause is:

The unit is one of the most dependable on the market

and the second is:

it is economical to operate

Both clauses could stand as separate sentences, with a period after each. Because the thoughts of the two clauses are closely related, however, the clauses were joined to form one sentence. Because the two independent clauses are connected by the coordinating conjunction *and*, a comma is used between them and is placed before the conjunction.

, *and* omitted

When two or more consecutive adjectives modify the same noun, they are separated by commas.

He was a quiet, efficient worker.

However, the comma is not used if the first adjective modifies the combined idea of the second adjective plus the noun.

She wore a beautiful green dress.

▶ Note: You can quickly determine whether to insert a comma between two consecutive adjectives by mentally placing *and* between them. If the sentence makes good sense with *and* inserted between the adjectives, then the comma is used. For example, the first illustration would make good sense if it read:

He was a quiet and efficient worker.